The Ford Foundation at Work

Philanthropic Choices, Methods, and Styles

The
Ford Foundation
at Work
Philanthropic Choices, Methods, and Styles

Richard Magat

PLENUM PRESS·NEW YORK AND LONDON

Library of Congress Cataloging in Publication Data

Magat, Richard.
  The Ford Foundation at work, philanthropic choices, methods, and styles.

  Includes index.
  1. Ford Foundation. I. Title.
HV97.F62M33   361.7'6'0973   78-24048
ISBN 0-306-40129-0

©1979 The Ford Foundation

Plenum Press, New York
A Division of Plenum Publishing Corporation
227 West 17th Street, New York, N.Y. 10011

Printed in the United States of America

Foreword

This report originated in a request to me from the Board of Trustees of the Ford Foundation in the summer of 1975. The trustees, aware that there would be a change of leadership at the Foundation before 1980, wanted to make a running start in the process of planning for the future. Their first step was to make a study of the great national and international needs that might lie ahead in the next decade and a half, and where and how the Foundation might address them. They sought advice both within the Foundation and outside it, and they engaged in long discussions of their own.

Although the exercise was directed toward planning for the future, the trustees also wished to review our past, not exhaustively but at least well enough to have a clear sense of what the Foundation had been up to in the quarter century of its existence as a national and international institution. In this connection, the chairman of our board, Alexander Heard, asked for "a canvass of the Ford Foundation's experiences, successes, and failures during the last twenty-five years . . . [focused] on the broad objectives sought, the means pursued to achieve them, and the results."

As policymakers for the Foundation, the trustees are ultimately responsible for the work of the staff, and they quite properly demand that we account for what we have done and explain what we would like to do. But I think it is fair to say that conversations between the Foundation's staff and its trustees are forthright.

So the report dealt with shortcomings, unrealized hopes, miscalculations, and downright blunders, as well as with what we regard as achievements. The writer of the report and those who assisted him also were free of constraints they might have felt if they were washing the Foundation's linen in public.

The review served its purpose well, and some trustees and staff members urged that we make it available publicly. We have decided to do so because it is as faithful a representation of what the Foundation thinks about itself as one can get in the circumstances. The changes made for this expanded public version consist mainly of eliminating institutional shorthand and spelling out references to matters that are familiar to insiders but that might be obscure to general readers. We also have omitted one or two comments that might unhelpfully reflect on the work of others.

This publication is meant as another step in a continuing effort to account for our work. We are required by law to record publicly what we have done. But it is a lot less clear to the public *how* we work, and therein, I believe, lies the chief value of this report.

The review shows how our objectives have been identified and also how varied kinds of action have been chosen. Along with careful and collegial designs, the reader will find choices that resulted from accident or personal inclination. These matters are illustrated by references drawn from our experience over nearly three decades. Obviously, the way we do our business reflects our own history and circumstances, and in publicly reviewing our methods and style of operation we do not imply that they are necessarily applicable to other grant-making institutions. The diversity among foundations is appropriate to the rich variety in the society that sanctions them.

Public accounting by established institutions is still dangerously limited in this country. As a result of the tempestuous events of the last ten or fifteen years, few of these institutions are now taken for granted. The hardiest of them have been questioned, even assaulted. It is altogether fitting that private institutions such as foundations be open to public scrutiny. But it is just as important that the examination of their affairs be informed. In the case of foundations, there has not been nearly enough informed analysis. For example, no full-scale history of the Ford Foundation exists, and we hope that perhaps this limited essay may stir some scholar or student to do that job. Although the task is more complex now than it would have been ten years ago, it is in some respects easier. The Foundation's archives have recently been assembled and opened to public use, under conditions that are unusually favorable. An oral history has been completed, from which more than two dozen interview transcripts are now available, and several more are to come in the next few years. Finally, the climate is more conducive to openness, in the society in general and in this institution in particular.

It remains only to thank Richard Magat for preparing this study. He has made our Office of Reports a model of responsibility and integrity, and I think readers of this study will understand why he is respected and trusted both inside and outside the Foundation.

MCGEORGE BUNDY
President
Ford Foundation

New York, N.Y.
February, 1978

Preface

The material for this report is drawn principally from the voluminous records of the Ford Foundation and from staff members' recollections (including my own, which cover twenty years of association with the Foundation). The first-person plural has been retained because another voice would ring false, given the manner in which the review first took place—the staff addressing the trustees. Since this report is now addressed to the public, readers may take "we" to mean the Foundation as a whole. Yet, the institutional "we" hardly means that the interpretations represent unanimity in a staff that is not wanting in independent spirits and diverse viewpoints.

Although I had the principal responsibility for preparing the report, dozens of staff members assisted. I am particularly indebted to Thomas E. Cooney, Jr., Oona Sullivan, and Willard J. Hertz. For her research assistance at all stages, I also am most grateful to Nancy Silbert. As in other undertakings, I benefited from the skills and goodwill of all my colleagues in the Office of Reports, not least those of my secretary Beatrice Toliver. It also was extremely helpful to have thoughtful comments on the manuscript from outside readers: Ben Bagdikian, Stephen Hess, Patrick W. Kennedy, John G. Simon, and B. J. Stiles. Many thanks are also due Mary Cox, whose firm, perceptive editing cleansed the manuscript of ambiguities and infelicities. Although this book incorporates many valuable suggestions from all these and others, the responsibility for any errors that may remain is mine alone.

I join Mr. Bundy in the hope that this publication may stimulate scholars to study the Ford Foundation. The Foundation once took the initiative in the preparation of a formal history, but the results suggest that the initiative had better come from another source. In the 1950s, the Foundation commissioned the late William Greenleaf, a former student of Allan Nevins, to write not only a history of the Foundation, but also a separate account of the founders' personal philanthropies up to the establishment of the Foundation. The latter work was published, and it is a lively and absorbing piece of scholarship.[1] Professor Greenleaf completed the history of the Foundation itself through the fall of 1956, but the commission had a string attached to it: the work could not be published without authorization by the Foundation. By the time he completed his work, a new administration was in place at the Foundation, and he was asked to wait. The history never came off the shelf, and, in any event, Professor Greenleaf had understandably gone on to other interests.

The only book-length account of the Foundation, Dwight Macdonald's adaptation of his New Yorker articles, was published in 1953.[2] That work is satirical, entertaining, and informative, but it is no more adequate today as an account of this institution than would be a popular history of the United States that ended with the Constitutional Convention in 1787.[3]

Oddly enough, there have been book-length studies of institutions created by the Foundation: the Fund for the Advancement of Education, the Fund for the Republic, and the National Educational Television and Radio Center. A few books about foundation

---

[1]William Greenleaf, From These Beginnings: The Early Philanthropies of Henry and Edsel Ford, 1911–1936 (Detroit: Wayne State University Press, 1964).

[2]Dwight Macdonald, The Ford Foundation: The Men and the Millions (New York: Reynal & Co., 1953).

[3]Two years ago, I was introduced to Macdonald at a social gathering, and I asked whether he had ever considered revisiting the Foundation and writing another book. He grinned and replied, with evident good nature, "I think I'll pass that one up."

philanthropy include fairly extensive discussions of the Ford Foundation. With one or two exceptions, they are more nearly popular journalism than informed analysis. In my view, much as I may disagree with some of his conclusions, Waldemar A. Nielsen's chapter on the Foundation in his book is the most balanced and authoritative account.[4]

Nor has there been a memoir of the Foundation, like Raymond B. Fosdick's valuable account of the General Education Board.[5] At least one man, many of us believe, was superbly equipped to do an illuminating memoir—William W. McPeak, who was staff director of the study that helped chart the course for the expansion of the Ford Foundation into a national institution and who later, for more than a decade, was a vice-president of the Foundation. But he died at the age of fifty-five, years before the time when a man who had committed enormous energy and intelligence to the life of an institution would have taken the time to look back reflectively and record its evolution.

So a task remains undone. The undertaking is important not because the Ford Foundation is the largest of its kind, but because its work has mattered in a number of developments in the social and cultural history of the latter half of the century. The most this report can do is to afford a glimpse of how such an institution has done its work.

RICHARD MAGAT

[4]Waldemar A. Nielsen, *The Big Foundations* (New York and London: Columbia University Press, 1972).
[5]Raymond B. Fosdick, *Adventures in Giving* (New York: Harper & Row, 1962).

Contents

Reviewing the Record

In this limited space, we shall try to illuminate the ways the Ford Foundation has carried out its work in the last thirty years. We will not attempt to summarize *what* the Foundation has done, for the record is immense—$5 billion in expenditures—and extraordinarily diverse—grants to 7,344 institutions, direct and indirect awards to more than one hundred thousand individuals, and activities in all fifty states and in ninety-six foreign countries.

To provide a brief historical context, the Appendix consists of a chronology; an outline of the fields in which the Foundation has been active, along with a list of selected major actions and a chart of total expenditures in each; and a chart of annual program expenditures.

In analyzing how the Foundation has worked, the review discusses the ways major objectives are chosen, the strategies and various modes of action most often used in the Foundation's attempts to achieve its objectives, and the results.

To illustrate the discussion, we draw heavily on particular examples from the record. Sixteen short case studies are included with this report, but other events in the Foundation's experience also are cited. We have selected the illustrations from various periods of the Foundation's history and from all of the broad areas of its interest, past as well as current.

A few words on the principal elements of this review may be helpful here, before each is discussed more fully in later sections.

OBJECTIVES

The Foundation was established in 1936, and, until 1950, it gave funds, averaging about $1 million annually, primarily to Michigan philanthropies. By that time, following settlement of the estates of the founders—Henry Ford, who died in 1947, and his son, Edsel, who died in 1943—it had become the largest foundation in the nation, with assets estimated at $474 million. Anticipating the transformation into a national organization of substantially greater scope and size than it had been in the 1930s and 1940s, the trustees in 1948 appointed an eight-member committee of independent consultants to chart the future of the institution. The study committee was chaired by H. Rowan Gaither, Jr., who later served as president of the Foundation (1953–1956) and as chairman of its board (1956–1958). Its recommendations, presented in 1950 in the *Report of the Study for the Ford Foundation on Policy and Program*, were adopted by the trustees virtually without change. The trustees then set forth in their own report five "areas for action" for which the Foundation would provide support:

1. Activities that promise significant contributions to world peace and to the establishment of a world order of law and justice.
2. Activities designed to secure greater allegiance to the basic principles of freedom and democracy in the solution of the insistent problems of an ever-changing society.
3. Activities designed to advance the economic well-being of people everywhere and to improve economic institutions for the better realization of democratic goals.
4. Activities to strengthen, expand, and improve educational facilities and methods to enable individuals more fully to realize their intellectual, civic, and spiritual potentialities; to promote greater equality of educational opportunity; and to

conserve and increase knowledge and enrich our culture.
5. Activities designed to increase knowledge of factors that influence or determine human conduct and to extend such knowledge for the maximum benefit of individuals and of society

These objectives were so broad and comprehensive that virtually everything the Foundation has done in the ensuing years can be rationalized as flowing from the original blueprint. (Among the few exceptions are our work in the arts, family planning, and the prevention of drug abuse.)

Near the midway point in 1962, the Foundation's objectives were restated, but they were still so comprehensive (and contained a loophole to the effect that the list was "illustrative") that they provided a shelter for all that we have done since and for virtually anything else we might have wanted to do.[6]

Although the present review discusses the way in which objectives have been chosen, we do not dwell on how rigorously the stated objectives have been pursued. For one thing, our announced goals have often been of a very high order of generality. A broad category such as "expanding individual opportunity and welfare" offers little helpful guidance to pragmatic philanthropy; it permits a near-infinity of laudable subgoals.

For another, much of what we have done has flowed not from objectives determined long in advance but from a variety of other circumstances. These include the pressures of changing events in American society and in the world, a mutation of work begun in pursuit of a stated objective, the persistence of an individual trustee, or the arrival of a staff member with rich knowledge of an important subject and a firm notion of how the Foundation could make an impact. These responsive actions range from *ad hoc* grants ($100,000 in 1959 for Governor Nelson Rockefeller's fallout shelter

---

[6]*The Ford Foundation in the 1960s*—Statement of the Board of Trustees on Policies, Programs, and Operations, July 1962. This report was the result of a two-year self-study. Many outsiders were consulted during the study, but the report was prepared by the Foundation's own staff.

program) to initially narrow grants that developed into important programs (e.g., our current ventures in neighborhood housing services and tenant management; see Case 11, p. 139). They include the creation of institutions with which we are glad to identify ourselves (e.g., the Drug Abuse Council, which was set up in 1972 as an independent national agency to fill serious gaps in society's effort against drug abuse; and the Police Foundation, which was set up in 1970 to support research and experiments in various cities to improve police patrol, criminal investigation, and crime prevention) and ventures we would rather forget (e.g., a costly and ill-fated attempt to establish a National Translation Center, $750,000, 1965).

This is not to denigrate the objectives our predecessors set. Thus, we believe that our support of studies of arms control (see Case 4, p. 111) and of the work of the U.S.–China National Committee falls within "activities that promise significant contributions to world peace . . ." the first of the "areas for action" of the 1950 report of the trustees, and that our support of Community Development Corporations is one kind of activity that can "advance the economic well-being of people . . ." (area 3). Community Development Corporations (see Case 6, p. 119), which have attracted major Foundation and federal support since the late 1960s, are locally controlled nonprofit corporations designed to deliver social services efficiently and to develop self-help programs in decaying communities. They seek primarily to increase jobs and income; to improve housing and to secure better services from local government, business, and utilities; and to foster a sense of hope in communities that have been stagnant or deteriorating.

Nor do we disparage planning and the positing of short- and long-term objectives. Indeed, through two-year budgeting and other devices, we are more deliberately foresighted than we were ten or twenty years ago. Rather, we wish simply to note here that we are flexible and that quite often our flexibility has permitted us to take action as the result of the pressure of events, the impact of individual personalities, and serendipity.

STRATEGIES AND MODES OF OPERATION

The longer it has worked, the more flexible and varied the Foundation has become in the way it works. The amount of money we pit against problems through straightforward grants is not necessarily the best measure of our effort. An informal conference that we assemble or a report that we commission can yield as much as a grant. The same may be said of individual consultations with government officials or of a joint venture with other foundations or international organizations. Occasionally, we use a new tool (e.g., program-related investments[7]) or assume a novel role (e.g., submitting briefs in proceedings of the Federal Communications Commission), but we also continue to employ long-established means, such as the creation of new institutions. Our efforts toward a particular objective also may be seen as a spectrum—from grants to individuals to institutional support, or from support of fundamental research to more operational activities, such as joint funding with public agencies or establishing organizations plainly committed to influencing public policy.

It is difficult to state flatly that one strategy or mode of operation works better than another. Thus, it sometimes seems wiser to help an existing institution overcome its weaknesses (e.g., our support of the National Committee Against Discrimination in Housing) than to mint a new one, but at other times it seems best to do the reverse (e.g., the creation of the Council on Library Resources). Also, the choice may be dictated by the stage of an effort: it was best at first to administer the Foreign Area Fellowship program ourselves (see Case 2, p. 97) but later to transfer it to the Social Science Research Council and the American Council of Learned Societies.

The way we do business also includes such internal activities and mechanisms as monitoring, technical assistance, evaluation,

[7]See *Program-Related Investments: A Different Approach to Philanthropy* (New York: Ford Foundation, 1974).

staff research, and use of consultants, advisory panels, task forces, and coordinating committees. A whole network of strategies, procedures, and instruments has grown in response to the enormous problem of selection faced by a grant-giving agency with a broad charter. There is no shortage of organizations, to say nothing of individuals, eager and qualified to address the problems facing society. For funds with which to carry on their efforts, institutions may turn to various sources—the public, the government, the business community, and their own members. However, the myriad needs of an increasingly complex world exceed the capability of even this array of funding sources. Thus, while the nation's foundations account for less than 10 percent of private philanthropic giving, the calls on their resources are enormous. The Ford Foundation alone receives more than twenty-five thousand requests each year—the great majority of them worthwhile—but our resources permit financing of only a small portion of them, usually less than 10 percent.

To make the best use of our resources, therefore, we need to pursue a systematic approach to grant-making. This means careful professional assessment of the intrinsic merits of all proposals considered for funding. It also means the concentration of our grants on a limited number of problems or objectives. Finally, it means an overriding concern for efforts of potential benefit to broad segments of society rather than to narrowly defined groups or limited geographic areas.

Less tangible elements of style also are important to an understanding of how the Foundation has worked. At various points in this review, therefore, we attempt to indicate significant organizational and atmospheric features—for example, the fact that we no longer interpret our independence to mean remoteness from what others are doing, the encouragement given to the initiatives of individual Foundation program officers, the collegiality within the staff and between the staff and the trustees, and the exchanges across departmental boundaries within the Foundation.

RESULTS

To the extent that this review deals with results, most of the judgments should be considered qualified. For example, we may feel very positive about the creation and nurturing of a new institution (e.g., the Mexican–American Legal Defense and Educational Fund), but this judgment should be tempered by asking why we did not get this job done five or ten years earlier than we did.

Also, it hardly needs saying that much depends on the beholder. We do not always have unanimity within our own staff on which efforts deserve A's and which F's. Once judgments are sought outside our walls, the variety of views is greater.

Another qualification concerns unexplored or foregone alternatives. To cite one example: In the 1960s, the Foundation made massive "challenge grants"[8] to private colleges and universities. The grants were to be used by the institutions in whatever ways they believed would advance their overall development. The amount and matching requirements of each grant were based on the size, programs, and fund-raising capabilities of the individual college or university. The grants totaled $349 million, and they drew an additional $1 billion to the institutions in matching funds. Most of these grants could be regarded as roaring successes in that they helped many institutions raise extraordinarily large amounts of new funds, they helped some colleges and universities develop into (to quote the program's lofty language) "regional or national centers of excellence," and they pushed many of them into the habit of systematic planning. But in hindsight, could we have used these same funds differently to improve the basic health of higher education?

Qualifications apply to negative judgments, too. We still think we were right in some general approaches even when we failed in

[8]So-called because of their matching feature, which was designed to stimulate contributions from other sources. See *Toward Greatness in Higher Education* (New York: Ford Foundation, 1964).

particular aspects. For example, we were right to have made innumerable grants to creative individuals in the arts, but when from 1960 to 1965 we awarded twenty-six poets and novelists fellowships totaling $227,000 to spend a year in residence with a theater or opera company, we were mistaken in hoping thus to create a whole new cadre of playwrights.

The results of some Foundation work can never be known comprehensively. Through scholarship, fellowship, and other individual-assistance programs, the Foundation has affected the lives of at least as many women and men as are graduated from a large university over a twenty-five-year span. We know that we played a part (through scholarships to leading ballet schools) in the education of Suzanne Farrell and Cynthia Gregory, currently two of the foremost American ballerinas, and we helped, through a $40,606 grant, in the completion of Professor Joseph Sax's seminal work on environmental law,[9] but to take the full measure, we would have to establish a large alumni research office. It would be nearly as prodigious a labor to trace the outcome of hundreds of small grants, although we can get an inkling of what we might find when we recall that a $23,000 grant in 1962 supported Charles Silberman as he wrote his prescient study of race relations, Crisis in Black and White[10] and that $64,000 to the United Nations in 1972 paid for the initial planning for the Conference on the Human Environment, which in turn led to the establishment of the U.N. Environment Programme.

In any case, the real credit for ventures to which funding sources like the Foundation point with pride belongs to the individuals or institutions that carry out the work. Another caveat about credit is in order. Here and there in this review, we report disappointment with a particular activity by one or another grant recipient. We do not invariably balance such particular illustrations with testimonials to the organization's general good work. So let us state at the outset that we do not intend any negative comment on

[9]Joseph Sax, Defending the Environment: A Strategy for Citizen Action (New York: Alfred A. Knopf, 1971).
[10]Charles Silberman, Crisis in Black and White (New York: Random House, 1964).

one piece of work to be taken as a general judgment on an organization.

Our accuracy in assessing the success of a given venture depends to some extent, of course, on the clarity of our reasons for undertaking it in the first place. Thus, it is relatively easy to rank as successful the Education program's Upper Division Scholarships for minority students[11] and the Arts program's effort to build up a handful of first-class resident theaters (see Case 8, p. 127). In contrast, final judgment will always be less precise on such efforts as the Gray Areas program. Its most visible measure of success was that it helped pave the way for one of the most important publicly supported social ventures in American history, the federal government's "war on poverty" in the 1960s. But a close analysis of its component parts reveals a mixed picture. It worked well in some cities, less well in others. Even in the cities where it was most successful, some parts of the program did not fare so well as others.

Clarity of objectives does not, of course, necessarily prevent failures. The Foundation's rationale for experiments with bullock-powered pumps in India was crystal clear, but it did not take long to learn that the idea was wrong.[12]

[11]The Upper Division Scholarship program, begun in 1970, was a national program to enable minority-group graduates of junior and community colleges to continue their education and complete the baccalaureate degree. Eligible black, Mexican–American, Puerto Rican, and American Indian students were nominated by the two-year institutions they had attended, and they used the scholarships to attend any senior college or university to which they could gain admission. The program, now concluded, totaled $7.5 million and assisted approximately 3,500 students from 1970 to 1976.

[12]The pump project (in Khanpur village, thirteen miles south of New Delhi) was part of an effort to demonstrate the small-industry potential of rural villages. It was hoped that the abundant animal power in Indian villages could be harnessed to operate a pump and an electric generator. Several small businesses (a woodworking shop, a blacksmith shop, and a brick kiln) were to be powered from the bullock-driven generator. The economic and engineering concepts underlying the project proved to be unsound.

Processes of
Philanthropic
Management

Before turning to the strategies the Ford Foundation most often employs in pursuing its objectives, it is worth reviewing the ways objectives have been chosen in the first place. These ways tell much about how the Foundation works.

It also may be instructive to discuss briefly the instruments and internal processes that the Foundation has used in carrying out its strategies. One traditional view of a foundation, held not only by cartoonists but by various persons-in-the-street and even by some members of the academy, is of a countinghouse to which proposals are brought to be sorted, one table for the rejects, the other for the accepted ones. This perception dies hard, but in fact, while some of our business *is* choosing among projects laid at our doorstep, we have become more sophisticated and professional in practicing philanthropy by taking our own initiatives.

CHOOSING OBJECTIVES

The changing patterns of Foundation activity reflect several influences. The 1950 report of the trustees established guidelines that at least in broad outline held for about five years. Although the original plan has become unraveled, some of its strands persist today. For example, on one of the resolves of 1950—"the reduction

27

of . . . racial barriers to equality of educational opportunity at all levels"—we did not make a forceful start until the middle of the 1960s, just as we were slow to support civil rights litigation (see Case 15, p. 154).

Generally, the major choices of objectives have been shaped by four influences: (1) the interests of individuals, ranging from trustees to staff, to say nothing of influential outsiders; (2) the force of external events; (3) substantial increases (and, more recently, decreases) in the Foundation's resources; and (4) the evolution of ongoing Foundation activities. These influences often overlap and interact; for example, the growth of drug abuse moved a single trustee to rivet the staff's attention to the subject.

In making choices, the Foundation recognizes that it is just one in a constellation of philanthropic institutions. Although we are sometimes the largest and most visible agency, we are never alone in working in our fields of interest. Indeed, as will be evident in the discussion of strategies, one of our major objectives is to identify institutions and individuals who are doing important work in order to assist them, collaborate with them, or help in disseminating the results of their experience.

The Influence of Individuals

In the beginning the trustees alone made most of the choices. They were guided in part by the 1948–1950 Gaither study, but their choices also reflected personal experience and proclivities. Thus, the presence on the board of the dean of a business school surely influenced our decision to support business education (see Case 2, p. 97), an activity we defined as falling within one of the five original areas of action, since it was "designed to advance the economic well-being of people everywhere and to improve economic institutions for the better realization of democratic goals." Just as clearly, the presence both on the board and on the staff of veterans of the Marshall Plan helped ensure our readiness, in the context of international relations in the 1950s, to support the Free University of Berlin and a wide range of institutions and activities associated with the strengthening of the Atlantic Community.

Some of the presidents of the Foundation, as they came on the scene, became major influences in certain choices; our interest in engineering education, for example, began and ended with Henry T. Heald, president of the Foundation from 1956 to 1965, and although we had supported certain strategic-studies centers since the 1950s, our current concerted support of analyses of arms control reflects a strong interest of McGeorge Bundy's. But under all the presidents the trustees have continued to be directly responsible for important initiatives, such as our entry into environmental conservation and our creation of the Police Foundation.

The staff itself is a source of new program ideas, although it also has the technical function of carrying out directives from the top. From time to time, staff members recruited for one purpose have made their mark in advancing and fleshing out an altogether different venture. The Foundation's initiative in the legal defense field, for example, was led by a man who began his work here with grants in the field of public administration. The staff member who first brought the Foundation into the New York City school decentralization maelstrom was initially hired to identify effective teaching practices in inner-city schools.[13] Sometimes, as in our work in school finance (see Case 12, p. 144), we were drawn to the subject by an outsider who was then hired to expand our activities. The shuttle of staff between the Foundation and the government has operated throughout our history. For example, it was a former staff member who, in a Washington assignment, first drew us into the housing field in the early 1960s. A decade later, primarily through the interests and experience of a newly arrived staff

---

[13]After the New York State legislature mandated decentralization of the New York City public schools and the city Board of Education authorized the creation of experimental school districts, the Foundation made grants in 1967 for three of the districts and subsequently for technical assistance to parent and community groups that had been given a greater participatory role in the schools. Decentralization was highly controversial and was accompanied by community strife and teachers' strikes.

member, we shifted our focus from low- and middle-income housing production to conservation.

In other instances, new officers or staff have turned long-standing activities into radically different channels. For example, the Foundation's new adviser on television changed the focus of our support in public television from individual stations and a limited national programming source to interconnected, simul-taneous national broadcasting. This new emphasis was coupled with a more realistic recognition of the cost of professional televi-sion program production and led us to sharply increase our budgets for public television for 1967 and for several years thereafter.

In much the same way, our support of higher education for minorities shifted over time. It had been an increasingly important part of our work in higher education generally, but in 1971 a new vice-president for Education designed a $100-million, six-year, minority-education program that took 75 percent of his division's budget.

It is hardly necessary to record that individuals outside the Foundation also have been prime movers in important choices. We were brought into cooperative education by an outsider (see Case 10, p. 135), and people in high places persuaded us to break our general rule against granting funds for buildings to spend $25 million for New York's Lincoln Center and $5 million for the John F. Kennedy Center for the Performing Arts in Washington, D.C.

Although we have not needed to advertise for outside peti-tions and advice, on several occasions we have deliberately invited a broad range of views on what we ought to be doing.

Events

Although we have continued to work toward a number of long-standing goals such as assistance to less-developed countries for nearly three decades, our agenda was reshaped by both gradual developments and sudden events in American society and in the world. We have sometimes been slow in responding, sometimes quick, and sometimes we have spotted small clouds that would develop into turbulent storms, as in the case of our Energy Policy Project in the early 1970s.

Also significant has been the influence of changing circumstances within fields in which we were already active. New actors have arrived on a scene in which we had been acting largely alone; the introduction of large-scale federal support of the arts and public broadcasting illustrates the point. Among other influences are altered social priorities and public policies—for example, the civil rights movement redirected the focus of our efforts in education. More recently, the growth of oppressive regimes in various parts of the world has led to a substantial increase in our support of agencies working to protect human rights.

The external climate does not always produce a constructive response, however. The Joseph R. McCarthy era and the congressional investigations of foundations took their toll of the Ford Foundation and no doubt helped to account for our caution, especially in the late 1950s, in approaching anything with great potential for controversy, and particularly civil rights. In 1952 Representative Eugene Cox of Georgia had led an investigation by a Select Committee of the House of Representatives of alleged subversive or Communist-influenced activities among foundations. The committee had concluded that the great majority of foundations were innocent of the charges, but it recommended that greater scrutiny of foundations be maintained. A follow-up investigation of foundations, centering on the Ford Foundation, was initiated in 1953 by Representative B. Carroll Reece of Tennessee, a former member of the Cox committee. Reece felt that insufficient time had been allowed for the Cox investigations, and he added a new charge, that foundation funds were being used for "political purposes, propaganda or attempts to influence legislation." The hearings of Reece's Special Committee to Investigate Tax-Exempt Foundations covered sixteen sessions from May 10 through June 17, 1954, amid sharp criticism in the press of the committee's methods of investigation. The final report of the committee recommended that foundations limit expenses by cutting their staffs and give up using "intermediary organizations" to distribute funds. A proposed federal law to remove trustees who made grants to "subversive organizations" was not acted upon. Two members of the committee, Wayne L. Hays and Gracie Pfost, issued a minority report condemning the committee for seeking to justify preformed conclusions.

The strong interest taken in our affairs by the Ford Motor Company during this period also should be noted. Until 1956, the Foundation owned 88 percent of the company's stock, and virtually all of the Foundation's income consisted of dividends from this holding. The trustees had felt for some time that it would be prudent to reduce the high concentration of the Foundation's assets in the stock of one company in one industry, and in 1956 a substantial portion of the Foundation's holding of Ford stock (22 percent) was converted into voting stock and sold to the public—the first public sale ever of the company's stock. Thereafter, the Foundation continued to diversify its portfolio, selling, granting, and exchanging 92.7 million shares of Ford Motor Company worth $4.2 billion. The Foundation completed divestiture in 1974.

Especially before the public sale of the company's stock, and thereafter to a lesser extent until we disposed of all our shares, some of our work drew strong objections from certain parts of the company. But it is well known among veteran trustees of the Foundation that Henry Ford II, the chairman of the company, steadfastly refrained from permitting his obligations to the company to interfere with his responsibilities as a Foundation trustee.

Changing Resources

Sometimes internal circumstances combine with external events and pressures to stimulate major new choices. The most dramatic example came in the mid-1950s, when the Foundation's Ford Motor Company stock was offered to the public. Although not required to do so at the time, the trustees decided that the windfall from this sale should be granted in a reasonably short period rather than added to the Foundation's assets. With the

Foundation beset by public controversy, the trustees also believed it desirable to make a highly visible public impression with safe and popular grants. The result was the $550-million Christmas package of grants announced on December 12, 1955:

1. A $260-million program to raise faculty salaries at private, regionally accredited, four-year, liberal-arts colleges and universities in the United States. More than 600 schools received grants under the program in 1956 and 1957.
2. Grants totaling some $200 million to approximately 3,500 voluntary, nonprofit hospitals in the United States and its territories. The grants, ranging from $10,000 to $250,000 and going to hospitals in virtually every congressional district, were to be used at the discretion of each hospital for improving its services to its community.
3. $90 million in endowment grants to 44 privately supported medical schools to help strengthen their instruction.

Similarly, a later bulge in the Foundation's assets was the primary motivation for our massive program of unrestricted challenge grants to private colleges and universities in the late 1950s and the first half of the 1960s; with our assets soaring over the $4 billion mark, we dusted off an idea that had been in one officer's drawer for years. In 1965, affluence also made it possible for the Foundation to commit in one swoop $80 million to symphony orchestras. For the last seven or eight years many major choices have been dictated by a contraction of our resources.

Evolution

Some of our most important choices and decisions have resulted not so much from an individual's initiative or the force of circumstances as from a succession of experiences that turned our work into channels distinct enough to be considered new phases or new fields of effort. The transition from the Gray Areas program to our concentration on Community Development Corporations is one example.[14] A more attenuated evolution is illustrated by our work in public broadcasting. Its seeds lay in efforts by the Fund for Adult Education[15] to respond to the call in the 1950 trustee report for activities aimed at "the more effective use of mass media, such as the press, the radio, and the moving pictures, and of community facilities for nonacademic education for better utilization of leisure time for all age groups."[16]

Without our experience in supporting legal reform and improvements in the administration of justice and our efforts to draw legal education closer to social needs, it is unlikely that we could have moved as definitively as we did into public-interest law. And our expansion of development assistance to Africa and to Latin America in 1959 and 1962 reflected two factors: first, the availability of substantially larger funds, and second, a belief that extending our overseas development activities would make more effective use of the experience acquired through our work in Asia.

PLANNING AND EVALUATION

We define planning as the process by which the Foundation staff chooses the range, beneficiaries, amount, and duration of philanthropic action after a general goal or field has been decided on. Planning can overlap the broader effort to choose objectives because we want to be assured by the design of tentative plans that we can act effectively in the new field.

Evaluation is the process by which we try to assess how well we have carried out an activity and what lessons we and others can draw from the experience. Normally, we distinguish between

[14]The term "Gray Areas" refers to urban sections likely to deteriorate into hopeless slums unless intervening programs are undertaken.

[15]The Fund for Adult Education was established by the Foundation in 1951 to assist experimental activities and to support promising programs in voluntary education after formal schooling. It was a nonprofit corporation with its own program, board of trustees, and staff. The fund ceased operations in 1961.

[16]For further information, see Ford Foundation Activities in Noncommercial Broadcasting 1951–1976 (New York: Ford Foundation, 1976).

"project evaluation" and "program evaluation." The first assesses the results of grants to particular recipients. The second takes an overview of an array of grants and other actions intended to serve a larger purpose, such as strengthening black colleges, promoting integrated housing, or making agriculture in India more efficient through water control. On a third level of generality—"strategic evaluation"—we try to determine whether the Foundation as a whole or one of its divisions has chosen the right priorities and balanced them properly. Evaluation in all three forms can, of course, overlap with planning; thus decisions to refund a grantee, continue a whole program, or adjust strategies often are affected by evaluations of earlier activities.

Planning

Planning is so pervasive and so bound up with other processes that it does not easily lend itself to taxonomy, but some principal ways in which the Foundation plans may be noted:

- The biennial budget process
- The presentation of information and action papers to the trustees
- Internally circulated staff background papers and memoranda
- Analyses, often involving outside experts, of fields in which we might become active
- Programs of exploratory grants
- Ongoing evaluation of grants and projects
- Staff conferences

Budget proposals and other presentations to the board are formal, almost constitutional, processes. The budgeting process demands from all the Foundation's divisions statements of projected grants and other actions and justifications of how these choices serve program goals. Credible and therefore explicit plans are required for the competition among divisions for the overall budget and for both new work and the continuation of current programs.

Information papers to the board often serve as dry runs for program plans. Many of these papers argue for entry into a field, and most also show in some detail what we would do if we were to enter.

Both on request and on their own initiative, staff members prepare many background papers and memoranda proposing actions and giving examples of grants to institutions.

Analyses and reviews, sometimes with outside direction or assistance, may be the most typical methods of Foundation planning. An example is the work of the Office of European and International Affairs in commissioning in 1972 a report on the international economic order.[17] The report proposed a broad research agenda, and one of the major responses by the Foundation was the establishment of a worldwide competition for research awards on international economic affairs.

During the period 1957–1962, the Humanities and Arts Division planned its basic fields of operation in the arts by means of exploratory grants. These tested whether or not individual awards to artists could be effectively placed and administered. They also helped determine the stage of career development at which the grants should be given. In addition to validating a jury system of awards and indicating that midcareer aid was the most effective, the grants gave the staff valuable knowledge, contacts, and experience. In a sense, all grant programs are exploratory because as they are evaluated at all levels of formality—from the mind of the program officer to a report by an outside consultant—their form and content are continually changed.

A great deal of collegial planning is done in staff retreats. Written presentations, oral discussions, and their after-hours extensions sometimes result in important innovations or changes. The International Division has institutionalized this device by convening worldwide meetings of its resident country and area representatives every other year; discussions at such a meeting in

[17]C. Fred Bergsten, *The Future of the International Economic Order: An Agenda for Research* (Lexington, Mass.: Lexington Books, D. C. Heath, 1973).

Kenya in 1968, for example, led to the division's broadened language activities in the developing countries beyond English-language training.

Perhaps the most formal, structured kind of planning is done in "formula" grant programs, such as the hospital and faculty salary grants of the 1950s, the symphony orchestra grants of the mid-1960s, and several fellowship programs in the Education and Research Division. Typically, these involve various mixtures of carefully stated eligibility requirements, criteria for selection of recipients, objective standards to determine the amount of each grant, selection boards, reporting procedures, and matching requirements.

Many of these modes and means have been used in planning to leave fields as well as to enter them. When the budget process involves drastic cuts, it constitutes a kind of reverse-gear version of ordinary program budgeting, as well as of most other planning methods. It also leads to a canvass of grantees heavily dependent on us, to assessment of the consequences of reducing or removing our support, to tapering schedules of decreasing grants, and to efforts to help grantees find other support.

Evaluation

The Foundation was late in instituting systematic evaluation of its work. Large programs were continued for many years without thorough assessments. Even before any formal evaluation had been made, decisions often were made to leave fields that the Foundation had supported extensively.

As noted earlier, major decisions may be made as a result of individual convictions or the force of external events; in such cases evaluation may not be an indispensable decision tool. Nor does an orderly assessment, even one that purports to be scientific, necessarily lead to the wisest decision. But, for obvious reasons, an institution like the Foundation should not neglect evaluation. It helps us to learn what we have failed to do or succeeded in doing, shows us how to avoid repeating mistakes, and aids us in accounting publicly for our actions. Finally, as a body of men and women who value the reasoning processes, we ought to prize analysis and reflection, of which evaluation is simply one type.

Evaluation has become an increasing activity throughout the Foundation, although still with considerable variation in kind and frequency. Project evaluation—directed at grants and series of grants—is basically a response to minimum requirements of law, procedure, and conscience, and it helps to develop a potentially valuable reservoir of experience. Suggestions have been made periodically that project evaluations be studied and discussed, but for the most part, these reports are prepared, collected, indexed, and placed in the archives to be consulted occasionally by the staff.

Project evaluation goes on in several forms. Recommendations for supplementary grants contain some assessment of the previous grant. Every formal "close-out" of a grant requires a program officer to commit to paper a judgment on the effectiveness of the grant. Also, each grantee is required to make narrative and financial reports each year and at the close of a grant.

Less *pro forma* and more elaborate are the frequent evaluations of major grants conducted by staff members (often other than those responsible for the grants) and by outside consultants and panels. There are no prescribed systems for deciding which grants get such treatment: the need is felt usually because of a sense that a grant has been especially effective or ineffective or because a decision on continued funding must be made.

A distinction should be noted between project evaluation and monitoring. The latter is the continuous process of surveillance carried on under the responsible program officer. Although it often involves outside consultants, this process is primarily a management aid; of course, it too yields material for evaluation.

Program evaluation—directed at blocks of grants and related actions that are aimed at a general philanthropic goal—is less frequent, more varied in form, and more ambitious than project evaluation. It is usually done on special assignment, by a staff member (or sometimes a former member), an outside consultant or team, or a combination of the two. Not all such evaluations are routinely circulated throughout the Foundation, but they usually are studied by those who had been involved in the program and by their superiors. Occasionally, and not only when they are favorable, they are published by the Office of Reports.

Subjects suitable for broader program evaluation are hard to find because we rarely are able to work in a field where the impact of our efforts can be clearly separated from other influences. Program evaluation is probably undertaken in vain when our work has been defined from the outset as a "contribution" to some major area of endeavor, such as engineering education or the Atlantic Community.

On a practical level, the basic issues of evaluation are these: How much evaluation should be done? How should it be done? Who should do it?

How Much Should Be Done? For years, most parts of the Foundation did little more than intuitive perfunctory evaluation. There is little question that with somewhat more formal assessments we would have been quicker to abandon costly, prolonged efforts that had reached or had even passed the point of diminishing return. For example, the hyperbolically termed "breakthrough" program in teacher education ($32 million, 1958–1967) consisted of a series of grants for experiments at 50 colleges and universities to improve teacher education. The purpose was to attract to the teaching profession superior students who otherwise might not have considered teaching careers in elementary and secondary schools. Most of the institutions in the program offered a Master of Arts in Teaching degree to liberal-arts graduates. Academic excellence was stressed, and efforts were made to provide extensive internships, sometimes paid, in actual classrooms. Although the program increased the numbers of first-rate teachers only marginally, it did underline the critical importance of training prospective teachers in schools and classrooms as well as in college courses.[18] It was

[18]See James C. Stone, *Breakthrough in Teacher Education* (San Francisco: Jossey-Bass, 1968).

clearly, though, a program in which we invested too much and which we evaluated too little.

Over time, as the Foundation has grown more professional and as society and our own conscience have pressed us toward a greater sense of responsibility for the consequences of our actions, we have moved steadily toward more evaluation. Still, most program staff have an entrepreneurial style; they tend to look forward, not back. And as a whole, the Foundation has been perhaps a little ingenuous in its implicit faith that the staff is routinely objective and self-critical. But as we have gradually increased our attention to evaluation, we have tended to create counterbalances to the institution's natural bent. Over the last several years the International Division has developed more demanding routines for evaluations when grants are closed out, and the National Affairs Division has maintained a separate staff unit for evaluation over the last nine years. The Education and Research Division is currently trying to build an evaluation system and simultaneously to raise the consciousness of staff on the subject.

How Should It Be Done? This issue overlaps the question of who should do it, except on one major point: Should evaluations be done quantitatively wherever possible? Social science has forged mathematically based tools of analysis that can be helpful in policy planning. Here and there we are trying to use them, but so far it appears to be no easier to identify our effect in a complex social system by traversing a jungle of measured but tangled variables than by more intuitive forms of analysis. Thus, the National Affairs Division found it hard to extract policy-relevant conclusions from an attempt by the Urban Institute to measure the local economic and social effects of Community Development Corporations.[19]

Who Should Do It? Insiders may be less objective evaluators than outsiders, but outsiders may have difficulty in learning what a project or program is all about. Usually insiders' biases are more

[19]Harvey A. Garn, Nancy L. Tevis, and Carl E. Snead, *The Final Report Assessing Community Development Corporations*, Volumes I and II (Washington, D.C.: Urban Institute, 1975).

easily identified and compensated for (sometimes insiders evaluating each other's work can be very objective indeed), and outsiders, out of self-interest, may try to tell the Foundation what they think it wants to hear. Authorities (usually outsiders) are often too committed or too specialized to be reliable evaluators in their own fields. Generalists can see beyond one field, and they are often useful in helping us cast a cool eye on the emperor's new clothes; if they have the analytical or investigative skills of good lawyers or professional reporters, they can be very helpful in all types of evaluation. But their lack of credentials in a field can be a drawback in getting specialists to make policy changes. The National Affairs Division has evolved a mixture in its own unit: an inside administrator selecting outside generalists and using them over and over again as they prove their abilities and their expertise.

The interplay between planning and evaluation was striking during the short period (1962–1965) when we had an Office of Policy Planning and Evaluation. Its missions were to aid the president in long-range planning, to prepare policy papers for the trustees, to interpret trustee policy to the staff, to oversee the budgeting process, and to conduct evaluations of projects and programs.

"Evaluation" was soon dropped from the title, but the office's staff continued to do *ad hoc* major evaluations, one of which—on Resources for the Future, Inc. (RFF)—illustrates the productive potential of evaluation. RFF, an independent national research institution with its own board of trustees, was established by the Foundation in 1952 to work on public policy formulation with respect to natural resources and the environment. In the review by the Foundation, it became apparent that although RFF was pursuing its research and policy objectives capably, other issues were developing—particularly those of ecology and environmental quality—that seemed to require more active Foundation attention. We explored these issues extensively with the aid of American and European experts, and the trustees decided to broaden the Foundation's own efforts in this field—a decision that led to what is now known as our Office of Resources and the Environment.

INSTRUMENTS

Although we have not employed any strikingly new devices in pursuing our objectives, we have come to use some traditional philanthropic instruments in more sophisticated ways. For example, we have increasingly moved away from paying grants in a single installment accompanied by a wave of farewell. We have learned to craft many grants so that payment or renewal schedules not only reflect shared hopes for the grantee's development, including hopes for infusions of additional support from others, but also serve as checkpoints on progress. In some instances, as in our work with resident theaters and ballet companies, the grant is part of a continuing relationship with an institution, including monitoring and technical assistance. Particularly in the case of organizations that depend heavily on our support, we often try to maintain helpful contact without intruding to the point of creating either overdependence or resentment.

Grants to individuals have become a major activity of the Foundation, greater in number, although not in expenditure, than grants to institutions. They have many uses, ranging from strengthening institutions by supporting their staff members (e.g., through fellowships) to explorations of fields for possible future Foundation action, and we shall discuss them in detail in a later section.

Some private foundations, such as the Twentieth Century Fund, the Russell Sage Foundation, and the Phelps Stokes Fund, work primarily by running programs themselves. For a variety of reasons, we have operated in the main by giving our money to others. As the nation's largest philanthropy, we have always believed that we can and ought to work in a number of fields. To do so by running our own programs instead of granting funds to others would reduce our ability to shift priorities or to leave one field after a period and enter others. Also, to run things ourselves as a general rule would contradict one of our important assumptions—that most of the fields in which we are active require extensive and diverse effort. When we have sometimes felt that no existing institution was capable of doing what was required, we have created a new one (as we shall discuss in the next chapter).

Still, our history is dotted with instances of our conducting projects directly. In much of our work in the less-developed countries, we have helped run various ventures as well as made grants.[20] We have maintained domestic staffs to administer fellowship programs, most notably the Foreign Area Fellowship program,[21] but also the Leadership Development Program,[22] the "forgivable loan" program in engineering education, and the programs of graduate fellowships for minorities. In addition, we have conducted or directly administered research, ranging from studies of income-contingent loans in higher education to an economic survey of the arts ($1.3 million, 1971–1975) and a review of reproductive biology ($300,000, 1973–1976).[23] But we regard such activities as exceptional. We expect them to be completed in relatively short order or to be transferred as soon as possible to others if a longer period of maturation seems necessary.

What has become more common is a role for staff that is neither grant-making, strictly speaking, nor operational, yet that serves program purposes. The role does not lend itself to a single

[20]Similarly, the Fund for the Advancement of Education and the Fund for Adult Education, both of which were wholly owned subsidiaries, were also mixtures of operations and grant-making.

[21]A $35.1-million program of graduate fellowships for United States citizens was established for advanced study on Africa, Asia, the Near East, Latin America, Eastern Europe, and the Soviet Union. The program was administered by the Foundation from 1952 to 1961, and has since been administered by the Social Science Research Council.

[22]The Leadership Development Program was designed to provide fellowships to rural educators and community workers who had leadership potential and a commitment to improving the region in which they lived. Grants for the program, which began in 1966, totaled $11.5 million through 1975.

[23]D. Bruce Johnstone, *New Patterns for College Lending: Income Contingency Loans* (New York: Columbia University Press, 1972); *The Finances of the Performing Arts: A Ford Foundation Report:* Volumes I and II (New York: Ford Foundation, 1974); Roy O. Greep, Marjorie A. Koblinsky, and Frederick S. Jaffe, *Reproduction and Human Welfare: A Challenge to Research* (Cambridge, Mass.: MIT Press, 1976); Roy O. Greep and Marjorie A. Koblinsky, *Frontiers in Reproduction and Fertility Control* (Cambridge, Mass.: MIT Press, 1977).

descriptive term, but it has elements of consulting, brokering, and entrepreneurship. For example, many staff members consult informally and are consulted by practitioners and policymakers in the public and private sectors. Armed with the reputation and resources of the Foundation and with their own experience and contacts, they can be helpful in drawing attention to issues, in enlisting the resources and efforts of others on priorities (see Case 1, p. 93), and sometimes in helping in the design of massive new enterprises in which our dollars play a small part or none at all (our work in cooperative education is an example here). Foundation staff members have also responded to requests for advice on legislation dealing with such matters as public broadcasting, manpower development, and legal services (see Case 3, p. 108). Some of our staff also have helped enlist international organizations and foreign governments in various enterprises (notably agricultural and population programs). Other staff members have worked successfully on philanthropic ventures with a range of businesses from banks to drug companies. Our staff has been looked to as a source of experience and advice by other philanthropic institutions, especially by new or substantially enlarged foundations, foreign as well as domestic.[24] The versatility of the staff roles reflects in part the growth of our professional staff, which nearly doubled, to 309, in the decade 1964–1973. But versatility also appears to have been maintained as the staff has shrunk (to 202 as of this writing).

Even when our staff was growing, we drew increasingly on the assistance of other groups and individuals to help us plan and administer our work. Since the early 1950s, we have used hundreds of consultants. In the early years, we used them primarily to help us review grant applications, and we continue to rely on peer review to an extent. But we have also used advisory bodies that help us develop new programs (e.g., in the arts) and panels of distinguished and respected specialists that not only give us sub-

[24]It also must be noted that we have sometimes given offense to other foundations; such complaints as overly demanding matching requirements, delays in making decisions, false encouragement, and bureaucratic procedures have been leveled against us.

stantive advice, but also serve as evidence of the care we take in working in sensitive fields (e.g., public-interest law).

One instrument we have employed more recently is the program-related investment. This is the use of capital funds to make loans to or otherwise invest in socially important, financially high-risk enterprises in various fields of Foundation interest. Since 1968, such investments have totaled $54 million, primarily in minority economic development but also in public broadcasting, housing, the arts, conservation, education, and community health. The device has been useful and the record quite good, considering the inherent risks. Either by choice or out of necessity, many grantees have learned to cope successfully with the business world and have become increasingly involved in large-scale projects aimed at fostering their organizational self-sufficiency as well as their social objectives. However, particularly in the area of minority enterprise, program-related investments have proved to be more complex than we had originally anticipated. Nonetheless, we expect to continue to use them to further an increasingly diversified range of program interests.

Strategies

The strategic approaches that the Foundation has taken in its work may be grouped broadly as follows:

- Building and improving institutions
- Generating and disseminating knowledge and information
- Developing individual talents
- Stimulating support from other sources
- Providing an independent contribution to public policy

Our characteristic behavior falls into one or a combination of these strategies whether we are working toward an objective set long in advance or, as noted earlier, responding to changing pressures or new opportunities. Consciously or unconsciously, we have used all these approaches, and whether one or another has attracted more support from us at one time or another has depended very much on the field and the project.

BUILDING AND IMPROVING INSTITUTIONS

The support of institutions is the way the Foundation has usually done its business. (For many years, "institution-building" was common terminology in the International Division's discussions of its work.) Also, half the funds given in support of individuals—for which more than 10 percent of our funds has been granted—have been given through institutions, some of which exist solely for that purpose (e.g., the National Merit Scholarship Corporation), while others have activities in addition to programs for individuals (e.g., the College Entrance Examination Board).

We have made *ad hoc* grants to individual institutions (e.g., $1 million to help convert the Rand Corporation into a private agency; $4.5 million for the development of Wolfson College, Oxford into a resident graduate institution emphasizing the sciences; and $94.8 million to the Henry Ford Hospital), as well as to classes of institutions (e.g., the $200 million program in the mid-1950s for voluntary hospitals). But most of our institutional grants are parts of larger strategies directed toward achieving our objectives. Thus, in addition to acting on appeals, we have taken the lead in establishing new institutions or reinforcing or attempting to reform existing ones (see Case 13, p. 147).

In aiding institutions, one of the principal distinctions we make is between support for particular projects and general support—the day-to-day operations of an institution. We have always been reluctant to give general support, but nonetheless we often have felt it important to do so, even to the extent of giving funds occasionally for endowment.

Among the recipients of general-support grants are some institutions that administer programs conceived by the Foundation. If the service these institutions provide is continuous enough, we have a vested interest in the institutions' efficiency and vitality. For example, we not only have given the Institute of International Education project grants to administer innumerable Foundation programs, but we also have granted it $7.1 million in unrestricted support to ensure its general capability. The American Council of Learned Societies has served as a major subcontractor for virtually all our work in the humanities ($43.7 million), for the bulk of our support of American studies in Europe (see Case 9, p. 132), and, in association with the Social Science Research Council, for East–West exchange programs and foreign-area fellowships.

Aside from the question of general support, the major recurring issues in our support of institutions are:

1. Whether to create new institutions or to work through existing bodies
2. The degree and duration of dependency of new or existing institutions in which we play a major role
3. The extent to which the Foundation can and should reinforce or attempt to redirect institutions
4. The nature of the institutions with which we deal (and particularly whether or not we have a penchant for "established" institutions that leads us to neglect the emerging, untried variety)

New or Existing Institutions?

In the Foundation's first years as a national philanthropy, it seemed that we were prepared to carry out our missions primarily by creating new institutions that themselves would work mainly by making grants to others. Thus, we established other foundations—the Fund for the Advancement of Education (established in 1951, supported by a total of $71.5 million), the Fund for Adult Education (1951, $47.4 million), the East European Fund (1951, $3.8 million), the Fund for the Republic (1952, $15 million), the Council on Library Resources (1956, $31.5 million), and Educational Facilities Laboratories (1958, $25.8 million).

In creating these new organizations we had several motives: a desire to keep the Foundation itself out of the "retailing" business; a hope that, especially in politically sensitive fields, a free-standing institution would have trustees who would be more authoritative sponsors of its work than our own could be; and a belief that a single-purpose foundation might better attract the specialized staff and leadership to carry out its mission than would a multipurpose one. (The notion of spinning off the International Division as a separate foundation cropped up occasionally in the Foundation's early years.)

By the mid-1960s, most of these separate foundations had gone out of business (the Fund for Adult Education and the East European Fund), had been absorbed into the Foundation proper (the Fund for the Advancement of Education), or had used all their Foundation funds and were attempting to function under other sponsorship (the Fund for the Republic). Some, however, remain to this day—for example, Resources for the Future, Inc., and the Council on Library Resources. Creating new foundations was our style in the 1950s in particular, but the past ten years have seen the Fund for the City of New York (1968, $10.1 million), the Police Foundation (1970, $25.9 million), and the Drug Abuse Council (1972, $8.8 million).

A related constellation consists of Foundation-created institutions that are primarily operating, rather than grant-making, institutions: the Mexican-American Legal Defense and Educational Fund (1968, $4.3 million), the Center for Applied Linguistics (1965, $6.7 million; see Case 14, p. 150), the Center for Advanced Study in the Behavioral Sciences (1954, $18 million), the Institute for Educational Leadership (1971, $5.8 million), and the Common Fund for Nonprofit Organizations (1969, $2.9 million). We would also include in this category institutions that existed in embryonic form but that might not have been born without our help—for example, the Native American Rights Fund (1972, $2 million), which grew out of California Legal Services.

Our current rule is that new institutions should be established on our initiative only when there is no acceptable alternative. Even when we ourselves see no alternative in a field, however, existing institutions in the field may argue that they could handle the work. Our reasons for feeling otherwise may include our doubts about the quality of leadership in an existing organization, a reluctance to make invidious choices among competing institutions, or, frankly, a desire to support an activity that relates to our own sense of need more closely than would be possible with an existing institution.

Occasionally we have worked the middle ground by placing an altogether new institution within an existing one—for example, the adoption of the Cable Television Information Center by the

Urban Institute and of the Educational Policy Research Institute by Educational Testing Service.

In a few cases, we have collaborated with other funding sources in creating a new institution. Sometimes the idea originates with another foundation (e.g., Carnegie Corporation's conception of the Children's Television Workshop), and we are then brought into the act. In other cases, we initiate the enterprise and bring others along (e.g., the Drug Abuse Council, in whose formation Carnegie Corporation, the Commonwealth Fund, the Henry J. Kaiser Foundation, and the Equitable Life Assurance Society joined us).

Where we have tried and failed to induce others to join us, we have sometimes gone it alone. Our experience in international language programs is a case in point, as is our lack of success in getting the federal government to join us in establishing an environmental policy institute, as we shall discuss later. Occasionally, new institutions emerge from programs we had run ourselves. For example, an intermittent series of grants for law school internships was transferred in 1968 to the newly minted Council on Legal Education for Professional Responsibility, to which we have since granted $11 million.

Despite disappointments along the way (e.g., the organization of Education and World Affairs and the Consortium for Educational Leadership), we have found the practice of creating new institutions to be worthwhile. We can never know surely whether or not assigning an activity to an existing organization would have been more effective than creating a new body, but we have a sense that most of those we have created have worked well.

Dependency

In some instances, the Foundation's support has been so great that both existing and new institutions have become heavily dependent financially. (It is worth emphasizing that in our relations with such organizations financial dependency does not—as far as we can avoid it—affect the independence of their managerial and programmatic decisions.) The number of organizations financially dependent on us has been declining in recent years. But there were dozens during the 1960s, including public-interest law firms, most of the community development corporations with which we were associated, many performing arts companies, and some public broadcasting organizations.[25]

There is a sense in which the relation between the Foundation and these bodies is one of interdependence. They have needed us, but we have needed their vitality to help us in our pursuit of program objectives.

We worry about the impact of claims from such "dependents" on our freedom of choice. This was a smaller problem five years ago than it is now, in a period of sharply contracting budgets; for example, 75 percent of the National Affairs Division's budget in 1978 and 1979 will go to activities that carry on earlier commitments. To retain a capacity for new ventures, we are exercising more care than ever in choices that create or perpetuate obligations to institutions that depend critically on our support.

Of broader concern is the quality of our relations with dependent organizations. How far does our responsibility go? Does our substantial investment in a venture make it difficult for it to obtain funds elsewhere? Does our strong interest in the success of an enterprise infringe on the integrity and independence of a free-standing institution?

In most cases, we believe that our relations with dependent institutions have been basically satisfactory. Where relations have been difficult from time to time, the issues have tended to be those of leadership (the Center for Applied Linguistics and the National Institute of Public Administration), poor focus (the International Legal Center), inexperience (particularly in fledgling minority institutions, such as the Southwest Council of La Raza), excessive

---

[25]Excluding the institutions cited, an internal study (September 1971) listed twenty-six organizations "whose existence depends in substantial degree on continuing grants from us." These were defined as organizations (1) that received grants from us at an annual level of $300,000 a year or more and (2) that depended on us for more than 20 percent of their basic expenses.

dependence (the American Council on Education in the 1960s, but no longer), or dissatisfaction by recipients of grants with our decisions or administrative processes.

We have shifted gradually from the view that once a grant is made we must leave the institution strictly to its own devices. We have learned that communication need not constitute meddling and that constructive examination is usually welcomed, not resented. We have learned to avoid many pitfalls of dependency by communicating better with grantee organizations and by intensive periodic review. It is dangerous to wait until the moment before grant expiration to assess the weaknesses and strengths of dependent organizations. If we had maintained a closer and more consistent overview of the International Legal Center, for example, it might have been possible for us to help the institution to make desirable changes earlier. Had we been in touch more frequently with the Adlai Stevenson Institute, we might have helped it avoid an invasion of endowment funds in direct violation of the terms of our grant.[26] However, it simply was not our practice to check into university-affiliated organizations under outstanding leadership and auspices more than once a year.

We also have learned that we cannot altogether escape identification with the unpopular actions of dependent organizations, even if our own role is small. We try to establish rules that will insulate the recipient institution from any temptation we might have to dictate particular decisions. Thus, we do not choose the cases undertaken by public-interest law firms or select the recipients of most of the fellowship and scholarship programs we

[26]The Adlai Stevenson Institute of International Affairs was founded in Chicago in 1967 as a nonprofit center to undertake research on domestic and foreign political, social, and economic development. The nucleus of its activities was a fellowship program for men and women in senior positions in public affairs. After meeting the matching provisions of the Foundation's endowment grant, the institute spent most of the $837,902 it received from the Foundation. When the institute dissolved, the balance ($146,994) was returned to the Foundation and regranted to the University of Chicago for the Adlai E. Stevenson Center, a successor to the institute. The center gives fellowships in international studies and sponsors lectures on topics of public and scholarly interest and symposia and seminars on international affairs.

finance. But when the Metropolitan Opera Company commissioned an opera about Sacco and Vanzetti, fire was directed as heavily at the Foundation as at the opera company.[27] We are prepared to accept criticism for our own decisions and to risk controversy when we think our objectives are worthwhile. We also may expect to be blamed for controversial decisions made by organizations we assist. Still we think it wise not to look over their shoulders every day. Actually, crisis and controversy have been very much the exception in our affairs.

Even in the absence of controversy, the relation between us and institutions we support is more complex than a "partnership," a pleasant term we are fond of using. We and they may be like-minded, but we have requirements and inclinations that may not square exactly with theirs. Furthermore, there is a sense in which they are client institutions. Our goodwill and high opinion are important to them. Even if we scrupulously avoid the clumsy use of our checkbook as an instrument of persuasion, the potential for misunderstanding and resentment is great.

Considering the great number of ventures in which we have been involved, there have been remarkably few instances in which we have had to take corrective action, such as requiring the return of funds, against grantees that have run afoul of either the law or the dictates of sound judgment. However, there have been instances in which we judged an activity to be so weak or so hopelessly storm-tossed that we have simply declined to give further support. Our withdrawal is sometimes dictated by a lack of effective program and management within a grantee organization. Difficulties have originated on our side of the table too—when we have not made our intentions clear in the first instance or along the

---

[27]The commissioning by the Metropolitan Opera of Marc Blitzstein to write an opera about the Sacco and Vanzetti case revived all the historical passions that have attended this highly controversial case. These passions were fanned by allegations that the composer had leftist associations. The Foundation, as a matter of policy, made no comment on either the choice of the composer selected by the Met or the composer's choice of subject matter. Blitzstein died before the opera was completed.

way, or when someone here has changed his or her mind, or when we simply have not thought through a venture adequately.

Even when grantee institutions have worked effectively, relations may be strained by questions of how long we should stay with an institution and how to terminate support. Such decisions depend on program objectives, budget restrictions, the breadth of the institution's capabilities, and a disinclination to cripple an organization by the abrupt removal of funding. For example, the Foundation supported a behavioral sciences program in the 1950s, granting some $24 million for basic and applied research, advanced training, and dissemination of knowledge about the study of human behavior. When the program was terminated in 1957, we made a substantial five-year grant ($5 million) to the Center for Advanced Study in the Behavioral Sciences, which had been one of the major recipients in the program. Although the center stretched these funds through the mid-1960s by gathering support from other sources, it then sent us a distress signal. The Foundation, then under a new administration, responded by granting another $7.5 million, part of which provides annual endowment income of perhaps $300,000 that will continue even after 1980.

We may well have stayed too long with some institutions we established, but there are often strong arguments for staying. Sometimes, to resolve the issue, we have made specific project grants after we have ended general support so as to maintain capabilities that have been built.

Some institutions continue to function under the leanest of circumstances, while others fall apart if we leave them. One of our most painful experiences concerned the Race Relations Information Center (RRIC), the successor to the Southern Education Reporting Service (SERS), which we helped establish in 1954 and to which we gave $2.2 million. SERS performed superbly in providing accurate, timely data on school integration in the South. From 1968 to 1972 we assisted its transformation into a national minority news service aimed at the white media. When we decided to go no further because of a shift to other priorities, the RRIC closed down.

While some institutions are genuinely dependent on the

Foundation (public broadcasting in its formative years), others are quasi-dependent; that is, they would lose some of their programs if we pulled out but would continue to exist (e.g., the Social Science Research Council and the American Council of Learned Societies).

Our support of financially dependent organizations is usually ended in one of four general ways: (1) through orderly liquidation (the North Carolina Fund, a nonprofit corporation established in 1963 to stimulate planning and experimentation on social problems and human resource development in the state); (2) by providing partial endowments to assure long-term financial security (American university centers of Asian and Russian studies); (3) by providing terminal grants for a transition period while other support is being attracted (public broadcasting); and (4) by merging the organization into other institutions (e.g., Education and World Affairs was absorbed by the International Council for Educational Development).

Sometimes we have left a field, comfortable in the expectation that our support would be picked up by others only to be compelled to return because of unforeseen circumstances, as was the case with international studies at American universities. We usually return on a smaller scale and at the same time make strong efforts to help attract funds to the field from other sources, governmental as well as private.

Reinforcement, Reform, Redirection

In many instances, our relations with institutions have been episodic or transitory. But quite often we have involved ourselves in the affairs of others both deeply and along a broad spectrum—from attempting to rescue faltering institutions to expanding and guaranteeing long life for some of the more successful ones. A preeminent example of the latter is the Brookings Institution. Twenty-five years old before the Foundation embarked on its national program, Brookings had built a notable record. We granted Brookings some $7.5 million for domestic and international projects from 1954 to 1965 as well as $6.2 million in general support. By

1964–65, our project and general support amounted to 45 percent of Brookings's annual operating income. At that point, we provided $14 million for endowment "in recognition of its emergence as a major resource for the nation's continuing quest for sound public policies." Altogether, including subsequent project support, we have granted Brookings $36 million.

Brookings never depended on the Foundation for its survival, but other established institutions might well have gone under in the absence of our support. The list of institutions to which we have given major reinforcement includes foreign area centers at several universities, the country's leading ballet and residential theater companies, a score of policy research centers, the principal public broadcasting production centers, major international agricultural research centers, and the legal defense funds of various minority groups.

We have frequently sought to reinforce whole classes of institutions—business schools, public-interest law firms, independent schools of art and music, and fair-housing agencies. Our presence is sometimes a counterbalance to views that would endanger certain types of institutions; a recent example was our large support for private black colleges ($50 million over six years) in the face of some opinion that they have outlived their usefulness. We have been less successful in reforming classes of institutions than in reinforcing them. We made a major effort ($10.2 million to forty universities) in the early 1960s to induce graduate schools to modernize the preparation of college teachers by strengthening the master's degree and accelerating progress toward the doctorate. Little changed for very long: many of the participating colleges and universities did not adhere to the substance of the guidelines, and many of the participating students did not place a high value on the master's degree as the ultimate credential for college teaching. The results of our more recent "doctoral reform" effort ($41.5 million to ten institutions, beginning in 1967) are not markedly better (see Case 2, p. 97).

In trying to rejuvenate weak institutions, we sometimes have set conditions we consider essential to their success, ranging from rethinking of purpose to structural reorganization, including key personnel changes. Whether or not our role has been resented has depended on such matters as our tact and the degree to which genuine dialogue has occurred. In the case of some heavily dependent institutions, we have proposed steps that transmuted them into entirely new forms. This was the case with the National Educational Television and Radio Center (NET), a program-production center to which we had granted $90.1 million over thirteen years. With the passage of the Public Broadcasting Act of 1967, the creation of the Corporation for Public Broadcasting, and the establishment of the Public Broadcasting Service as the national networking organization, the center lost many of its functions, and its role had to change radically. Therefore, we encouraged it to merge with the Educational Broadcasting Corporation, operator of New York's public television station, which was in need of the kind of programming capacity NET had.

Under our prompting, a less drastic reorientation was effected in 1975 by Resources for the Future. Among other things, RFF undertook aggressively to diversify its funding and to reduce its dependence on the Foundation; whereas nearly 90 percent of its funding had once come from the Foundation, by 1977 the figure was reduced to 66 percent and is expected to drop to 48 percent by 1979.

Yet, we do not always intervene in organizations in which we have a large investment. Once in a while, we have wished that the leadership of certain recipient institutions were different but have felt it unwise or impolitic to attempt to do much about it.

Established and Nonestablished Institutions

Some critics have accused the Foundation of trafficking only with established institutions, with the implication that we are essentially maintaining the status quo. Two observations may be made on this score.

First, what is "established" is not necessarily static (to the example of Brookings one may add renowned universities that have responded nimbly to changes in society and in knowledge).

Second, especially since the mid-1960s, we have done business with innumerable "nonestablishment" institutions, some already in existence, others that we helped to create.

We are not likely to be free of the issue of favoritism toward established institutions so long as critics at the ideological poles consider the Foundation itself a member of the establishment. But we think the issue is insubstantial and, furthermore, clouded by differing definitions and perceptions. For example, the age of an institution is not a necessary determinant of established status. By almost anyone's reckoning, organizations like the Urban Institute, which over the last ten years has become a major producer of policy-related social and economic research on urban problems, become "establishment" the day they incorporate because of their auspices. Conversely, many radical organizations on the left and right that have been around for a long time remain "nonestablishment." Nor do our own criteria alter the perception of others; the literary establishment of the *New York Review of Books* and *Commentary* might not consider the American Council of Learned Societies part of *the* intellectual establishment, but we do.

We should not be surprised that the "establishment" critique dies hard. Early in our history as a national institution some Foundation officers and staff believed in the trickle-down approach in many fields. It was not so much that it was the safest thing to do, but that it seemed the most natural and effective course. "Excellence" was our watchword, as well as John Gardner's.[28] For nearly a decade, for example, we made many attempts to reform public education through support of universities and other external agencies, and for years our approach to enhancing economic well-being

---

[28]John Gardner, while president of Carnegie Corporation, wrote a widely noted book, *Excellence: Can We Be Equal and Excellent Too?* (New York: Harper & Row, 1961) calling for very high levels of competence in all walks of life. He later became Secretary of the U.S. Department of Health, Education and Welfare.

in the United States lay in our support of leading business schools and talented economists.

Taking our history as a whole, we have in fact dealt in domestic affairs primarily with established institutions. Of the some 2,500 domestic institutions we have supported, only 65 have received $10 million or more, but the grants to these institutions account for nearly three-fourths of the funds we have spent in the United States. Half of the 65 largest recipients are leading colleges and universities.

But increasingly, and for quite some time now, our attitude may be described as pragmatic. The quality of an institution's work—what it is capable of doing to further objectives we consider important—matters more to us than its status.

So we are not insensitive to the risk of ignoring all but the tried and true, and occasionally, that sensitivity has played a part in our decisions. Consider these two examples:

The $8.5-million Venture Fund program, established by the Foundation in 1970 to encourage innovation in undergraduate education, was deliberately set up in such a manner that out-of-the-way places could qualify. Venture Fund grants enabled college presidents and liberal arts deans to finance special projects for which regular budget funds would not have been available, or to respond quickly to good ideas. Such grants were made to 49 colleges and universities in the United States between 1970 and 1974.

Through a cash reserve program in the arts, begun in 1971, we have assisted more than twice as many performing arts organizations as we had in the previous 15 years of working very selectively. The program sought to attack two recurring problems of performing arts organizations—cash flow and net current liabilities. Each cash reserve grant is made on a one-time, nonrenewable basis. As of the end of 1977, $25.8 million had been granted to 63 performing arts organizations under the program.

Other examples are the previously noted large formula programs for hospitals and the improvement of faculty salaries, and a ten-year, $80-million program for 61 symphony orchestras throughout the country.

GENERATING KNOWLEDGE FOR UNDERSTANDING AND ACTION

However badly rationality may have fared in the world in the last quarter century, the Foundation has maintained faith, although not blind or boundless faith, in the value of knowledge. We are convinced that lack of knowledge and understanding impedes progress in virtually all matters with which we deal. And so research support is one of our major strategies.

In this discussion, we use "research" as shorthand for a range of activities from scholarly inquiry to homely fact-finding and assembly of data and the dissemination thereof. Put another way, as we did twelve years ago in announcing a major commitment to minority opportunity: "Research is a heavy word for a kind of work which can be described in clear, lighter, simpler words: to learn and tell the truth."

The Rationale for Research and Fact-Finding

Sometimes we support research and information-gathering efforts because they are the most promising way to get at a problem, because they are a necessary prelude to action by ourselves or by others, or because they can help draw attention and resources to neglected problems.

As we become interested in a subject, often one of the first things that strikes us is how little is known about it. That perception may reflect the natural protective caution (or call it professional prudence) of people responsible for handing out large sums of money. We hesitate to take action until we have a reasonably clear idea of the nature of the problem that the money is intended to help resolve. The Foundation has therefore turned to studies, investigations, and reports—not simply to fill gaps in knowledge, but also to advance understanding to the point at which either we or other private or public agencies feel more confident about taking action.

We also have occasionally commissioned studies of the "state of the art" in particular research fields. Examples include the Lindbeck report on China studies,[29] the Bergsten report on the international economic order,[30] and a conference on research into television's effects on children.[31] And we have, although more rarely, conducted research internally: as a prelude to supporting experiments by others (e.g., an information paper on white ethnic and working-class people, "The Suddenly Remembered American"); to clarify issues we have raised (e.g., the legal and financial studies of college endowments),[32] or, as in our study of the economics of the performing arts,[33] to help government and other private donors target their aid more precisely.

Support of research comes naturally to a private foundation. For one thing, a foundation often is a first or last resort for research that cannot or should not be supported by other sources, commercial or governmental. Also, while it is still possible for foundations to make an effective contribution by launching or assisting pilot programs, experiments, and demonstration projects, the sheer scale of need precludes foundations in the late twentieth century from conducting very many large action programs, as the Rockefeller Foundation was able to do in rural public health around the turn of the century.

In supporting research generally, our strategic motivation has

[29]John Lindbeck, *Understanding China: An Assessment of American Scholarly Resources* (New York: Praeger, 1971).

[30]C. Fred Bergsten, *The Future of the International Economic Order* (New York: Ford Foundation, 1973).

[31]*Television and Children: Priorities for Research* (New York: Ford Foundation, 1975).

[32]William L. Cary and Craig B. Bright, *The Law and the Lore of Endowment Funds* (New York: Ford Foundation, 1969); *The Developing Law of Endowment Funds: The Law and the Lore Revisited* (New York: Ford Foundation, 1974).

[33]*The Finances of the Performing Arts* (New York: Ford Foundation, 1974).

varied greatly. We supported the behavioral sciences in the 1950s and early 1960s because we thought they were relatively neglected. The Gaither report had stated, "the evidence points to the fact that today's most critical problems are those which are social rather than physical in character—those which arise in man's relation to man rather than in his relation to nature. Here, it was concluded, is the realm where the greatest problems exist, where the least progress is being made, and where the gravest threat to democracy and human welfare lies." We supported economics in that period not because it was a neglected field, but because we believed it could make a greater contribution than it was making. More recently, our support in such areas as criminal justice, reproductive biology, and school finance has stemmed from a judgment that knowledge in these areas is thin and that effective action requires a quantum increase in the intellectual effort invested in them. Research is a major strategy in our work in the developing countries. Through support of individuals, institutions, and research communities, we have tried to help these countries build a research capacity in agriculture, population studies, and economics and the other social sciences so that they may take intelligent, sustained action on development problems.

We have been responsible for some highly visible studies that sought to draw attention to an issue: *The Negro and the Schools;*[34] *With All Deliberate Speed,*[35] a study of the slow pace of desegregation; a report on *India's Food Crisis and Steps to Meet it;*[36] James Bryant Conant's *Slums and Suburbs;*[37] Charles Silberman's *Crisis in Black and White;*[38] and Earl Cheit's *New Depression in Higher Education.*[39]

In some cases, our research support in a comparatively ne-

[34]Harry S. Ashmore, *The Negro and the Schools* (Chapel Hill: University of North Carolina Press, 1954).
[35]Southern Education Reporting Service, *With All Deliberate Speed,* Don Shoemaker, ed. (New York: Harper, 1957).
[36]Agricultural Production Team, Report on *India's Food Crisis and Steps to Meet It* (Delhi: Government of India, 1959).
[37]James B. Conant, *Slums and Suburbs* (New York: McGraw-Hill, 1961).
[38]Charles Silberman, *Crisis in Black and White* (New York: Random House, 1964).
[39]Earl Cheit, *New Depression in Higher Education* (New York: McGraw-Hill, 1971).

glected field—reproductive biology, for example—has helped to attract new talent, to encourage established scholars to direct their expertise to solving problems in the field, and to draw new resources, particularly large-scale government funding, into advancing the work.

We also have supported research that aims to intensify work on problems by illuminating them more sharply. Thus, our long-term support for demographic research is intended to stimulate the movement toward limiting the world's population growth. Shorter-term examples include studies such as the Meyerson Commission report on higher education,[40] the tenure study by the Association of American Colleges/American Association of University Professors,[41] and Silberman's current analysis of crime in the United States.[42] The crime study is not intended mainly to draw attention to a subject about which most of the country is already exercised. Rather, it seeks to further understanding of the manifold causes of lawlessness so that more effective preventive measures may be devised. Similarly, we saw psycholinguistic surveys conducted under our international language programs as indispensable to understanding the kinds of language problems—in their social and psychological as well as their purely linguistic dimensions—that exist in the countries in which we work.

Characteristics of Research Support

Range. Our research support has covered such a broad spectrum that there are not many fields in which we have not been active at one time or another. At one end, we have supported research in the humanities (e.g., history and archaeology), at the

---

[40]Assembly on University Goals and Governance, *First Report of the Assembly* (Boston: American Academy of Arts and Sciences, 1971); "American Higher Education: Toward an Uncertain Future," *Daedalus*, Fall 1974 and Winter 1975 (second report of the Assembly on University Goals and Governance).

[41]Commission on Academic Tenure, *Faculty Tenure* (San Francisco: Jossey-Bass, 1973).

[42]Charles E. Silberman, *Criminal Violence, Criminal Justice* (New York: Random House, 1978).

other, the natural sciences (reproductive biology and, for a short period, plasma physics and the atmospheric sciences). In some research fields (criminal justice, agriculture in the less-developed countries), our support has played a critical role.

Our methods of support also have been varied. Assistance has been given to individuals ranging from leading scholars to graduate students. We have supported established research centers and new ones, and we have sustained research networks and institutions that stimulate and coordinate research (e.g., the Social Science Research Council and the Population Council). In some instances, we have bypassed the instrument of project support and have tried, instead, to develop research capacity in a field as a whole (e.g., molecular biology). In addition, we have sought to strengthen adjuncts to scholarship through support of university presses, scholarly journals, archives, and special collections. Parallel to building general research capacity in neglected fields, we have supported a vast array of research on particular issues and problems. Over the years, we have underwritten studies on topics ranging from linguistics to the common problems of advanced industrial societies; from library resources to arms control; and from increasing the efficiency of police patrols to improving strains of wheat.

Independence. Paucity of research by others has not been the sole criterion for our decisions to support various lines of inquiry. The volume of research on drug abuse, for example, was already large when we established the Drug Abuse Council. Here we acted on the conviction that only an independent agency like the council could produce the kind of disinterested research and analysis that could command widespread support in a field racked by uncertainty and contention. In the six years that the Drug Abuse Council has been at work, this view has been confirmed by virtually all concerned. The advantages of independent inquiry also prompted our support of such undertakings as a recent comprehensive study of nuclear energy.[43] And we have provided an extra measure of

[43]Spurgeon M. Keeny, Jr. *et al., Nuclear Power Issues and Choices* (Cambridge, Mass.: Ballinger, 1977).

independence by helping to support inquiries initiated or supported principally by others, as in our grants ($640,000) for special
studies required by the U.S. National Advisory Commission on
Civil Disorder but either not covered by its federal appropriation or
inappropriate for government sponsorship, and grants totaling
$58,000 for studies on the implications of Watergate.[44]

Some other characteristics of our support of research are worth
noting:

> Research often is built into multipurpose grants.
> Sometimes simple fact-finding serves as the bridge to
> important innovations; data assembled by the Vera In-
> stitute of Justice on arrest and release practices (origi-
> nally with the support of Louis Schweitzer, the philan-
> thropist who founded the institute) were the necessary
> prelude to the cooperation of the courts and the police in
> experiments that led to reforms in the bail and sentenc-
> ing systems. Similarly, patient, slogging fact-finding
> supported by the Fund for Adult Education provided
> the irrefutable evidence in the early 1950s that helped
> persuade the Federal Communications Commission to
> set aside a significant part of the broadcast spectrum for
> noncommercial broadcasting.

> In just about all our research support, we add an
> extra dollop of funding to disseminate the results and
> thus to advance public understanding of the issues. As
> an integral part of support for several American Assem-
> bly programs on a wide range of issues, we financed
> publication of the concluding reports. (The assembly, an
> affiliate of Columbia University, is a national forum for
> discussion of major topics of national concern; it aims to
> achieve consensus among a selected group of particip-
> ants chosen for geographical balance and representation

---

[44]Alexander Bickel et al., Watergate, Politics, and the Legal Process (Washington, D.C.:
American Enterprise Institute for Public Policy Research, 1974); Frederick C.
Mosher, Watergate: Its Implications for Responsible Government (New York: Basic
Books, 1974); Ralph K. Winter, Jr., Watergate and the Law: Political Campaigns and
Presidential Power (Washington, D.C.: American Enterprise Institute for Public
Policy Research, 1974).

from business, the professions, government, and the field most closely associated with the topic of discussion.) And as an extension of efforts to improve state legislatures and public understanding of state government ($21 million over a period of nineteen years), we funded three monthly magazines devoted exclusively to state government affairs in California, Illinois, and New York.

Issues in Research Support

Timeliness. In any effort to focus wider attention on the importance of a problem, timing is crucial. It is not necessary for the Foundation to be first into the pool, but opportunities for service may be irretrievably lost if we wait until a half hour before closing. We often have moved in timely fashion and by doing so have given an issue wider attention than it had enjoyed. Such has been the case with our work on the problems of white ethnic communities, working-class issues, and occupational safety. When attention to these areas was beginning to grow, we acted promptly to support research and disseminate the results and to sponsor such programs as worker exchanges and workplace experiments, all of which were aimed at more clearly defining the issues and advancing understanding of them.

Sometimes we have been tardy, and we have not always been immune to social and political pressures for delay. However, in any number of other instances, we have anticipated needs and supported research and other activities accordingly. And we also respond to current, commonly held concerns: when uneasiness about campus disruption, welfare costs, or crime runs high, we try to see if there is a role we can play.

Occasionally we have entered well-plowed research areas, stayed for a while, and produced little of importance, as in the various commissions on student unrest we supported with some $100,000 between 1968 and 1970 and a $7-million series of grants for delinquency research in the 1950s and 1960s. (Youth research centers that we established at Syracuse University and at the University of Southern California were productive, although the latter folded after our funds ran out.) Sometimes our joining in turns out to be worthwhile (manpower, drug abuse, and agriculture).

At times, when we have acted somewhat in advance of the rest of society, we have found our efforts coinciding fortuitously with events. The Foundation's Energy Policy Project was organized more than a year before the Middle East oil boycott that triggered the "energy crisis." The purpose of the project was to illuminate a range of energy issues, encourage public discussion, and help set the stage for the formation of new national energy policies. Few of the studies were in hand or published when the crisis broke, but the public hue and cry over the oil shortages whetted appetites for our reports as they appeared. The final report, *A Time to Choose: America's Energy Future*,[45] received far more attention than it otherwise would have. In the ensuing years, its basic findings have gained in acceptance, and several of the supporting studies are contributing to the formation of a comprehensive national policy of which energy conservation is a cornerstone.

Favoritism. The question of whether or not we are fair in our choice of research subjects, individual scholars, and institutions has arisen, but, considering the range of research we have supported, not very often. Occasionally (less so in recent years), we have added our two cents to the support of noted investigators (the Piagets and Leontiefs of the world) because we thought we could help them make even richer contributions. More often, however, we have sought top talents because we hoped to get a particular job done. But we do not anoint mainly the senior investigator. In the 1950s, we may have had a penchant for establishing professorial chairs (which in certain fields at certain times is one of the best possible ways of advancing knowledge), but even then, and especially since then, we also have supported innumerable fellowship programs for fledgling researchers, and the directors of particular research programs have ranged from men and women in their thirties to senior-citizen scholars. Also, in some research competitions, we limit the nominations from any single institution.

[45]*A Time to Choose: America's Energy Future* (Cambridge, Mass.: Ballinger, 1974).

But perhaps our greatest sensitivity to the need for balance is displayed in the efforts we and our grantees have made, especially in the last several years, to draw from a wide political spectrum in the composition of boards of trustees, advisory bodies, major conferences, workshops, American Assemblies, and other forums.

Fundamental Research. In a number of areas, the research we support is so finely targeted that it falls outside most definitions of "fundamental." Whereas once our support of "research on government" consisted in great part of filling chairs in political science, more recently it has dealt with such activity as the evaluations of federal manpower programs by Sar Levitan of George Washington University or the work by the Southern Regional Council and citizens' groups in monitoring government performance in revenue-sharing and other specific legislation. Nevertheless, we have not ignored support of basic research: we gave the Institute of Advanced Study at Princeton $1.5 million in 1969 to start a new school of social sciences; we have contributed to research on learning by Jerome Bruner and Jean Piaget; and our support for fundamental reproductive science has been considerable. These examples by no means exhaust the list.

Still, although we do not fret much about the well-worn argument over pure versus applied research, we have tended to hope that even the basic research we support will pay off sooner rather than later. The $42.8-million Behavioral Sciences and Mental Health program—most of it in support of basic research—was a response to the decision by the trustees in their 1950 report that one of the Foundation's five broad areas for action should be support of "scientific activities designed to increase knowledge of factors which influence or determine human conduct" *and extension of such knowledge "for the maximum benefit of individuals and society"* (emphasis added). In underwriting research into the fundamental processes of the reproductive system, we are anticipating that some of the results will lead to better contraceptives. In assisting the learning research of Michael Cole at the University of California (San Diego), we hope that some day the outcome will help teachers and pupils of diverse backgrounds to understand one another better and thereby improve children's education.

Our view of fundamental research also reflects changes in supply and demand; thus, although most of the agricultural research we have supported has been applied, we are beginning to recognize that in seeking solutions to serious problems the international agricultural research centers have exhausted most of the available basic research, and we are now considering whether or not we should provide support for such further fundamental research as studies of photosynthesis.

As our staff's professional skills have sharpened, as public and other private sources of funding for basic research have grown, and as (at least in some of our domestic divisions) we have been disappointed in the results of some research we have supported in the past, we are inclined to support fundamental research only if it seems to be a prerequisite to getting on with the job of solving a particular problem. "In other words," as one of our officers has put it, "we support problem-oriented fundamental research." In our work on the international economic order, for example, we deliberately include support for fundamental research because we believe it is needed before the problem can be dealt with.

Research versus Action. To put research and action in opposition is in some respects fallacious. It implies that support of research is an escape from supporting action in a given situation. In some matters—peace, for example—research (and dissemination of the results) may be the only practicable avenue for our participation. In other instances, we believe that we are lacking sufficient knowledge on which to base constructive and effective action. For example, we declined to support activism on the question of post-Vietnam amnesty in favor of a comprehensive study of amnesty and veterans' affairs generally.[46] Yet, we have sometimes stuck to the research path when we could have supported some programs of action. Through most of the 1950s, for example, our interest in urban problems was channeled primarily into support of a series of

[46]Lawrence M. Baskir and William A. Strauss, *Reconciliation after Vietnam: A Program of Relief for Vietnam-Era Draft and Military Offenders* (Notre Dame, Ind.: University of Notre Dame Press, 1977).

research studies on, for example, regional economics, housing, and metropolitan government.

Finally, in many fields, we have supported research and action simultaneously. At the same time that we financed reproductive-biology laboratories, we assisted family-planning programs. Even as we expanded work in learning research, we continued to support experiments and demonstrations in teacher-training and alternative schools. Similarly, we support not only research on integrated education and community efforts to facilitate implementation of court orders to desegregate schools, but also civil rights litigation (along with backup research).

We are not unmindful of the impatience with research, especially in matters marked by persistent or growing crisis. We sometimes share the skepticism of "studies that lead to more studies," as a recent evaluation of a long-time grantee put it. But we believe it is as simplistic to suppose that effective action can proceed without knowledge as it is to believe that research is a substitute for action. There are few simple answers to anything, and research helps avert the application of simplistic or disastrously wrong answers to large and complex questions.

DEVELOPING INDIVIDUAL TALENTS

In the broadest sense, assistance to individuals underlies all our activities. Whether we are trying to help reform institutions, generate knowledge, or affect public policy, we depend on the talents and energies of the individual scholars, specialists, artists, or students involved in the programs we support.

More specifically, however, we have made thousands of grants directly for the development of individual competence or for the encouragement of research by individuals in neglected or underdeveloped fields. These grants have been highly diverse, depending on such factors as the problem addressed, the geographic area affected, the existing level of competence in a region or discipline, and, above all, the Foundation's objectives. Thus, we have supported the advanced education of behavioral scientists and foreign-area specialists to prepare them for academic careers; the preparation of minority-group members for leadership in such fields as law, education, and business; the training of agricultural technicians and economic planners for nation-building work abroad; and individual research projects on problems of the environment, economic growth, and public policy.

As broad as our support for individuals has been, the exclusions have necessarily been greater, reflecting both our finite financial resources and our program priorities. As a matter of policy, the Foundation has generally avoided support of individuals in the physical sciences (with the exception of such programs as science and mathematics education in developing countries and our limited domestic Science and Engineering program, 1958–1966), health and medicine (except as they relate to population problems), or religious activities. Nor do we respond favorably to the hundreds of requests received each year to meet personal needs or alleviate personal distress. Even in our assistance to refugees, which totals some $7.7 million, we have concentrated on intellectual and professional leaders in fields that fall within our program interests. Nonetheless, it is a fact that individuals can and do call upon the Foundation for assistance, and in recent years hundreds of individual grants have been awarded in the United States annually. The number of applications is, of course, much larger. Also, given the fact that grantees award most grants to individuals, the seeker of assistance is well advised to consult standard sources of federal and private fellowships, scholarships, and grants to individuals.

In general, our efforts on behalf of individuals fall into two categories: (1) development of the institutions needed to identify and train talented individuals in certain specialties or for work on specific problems; and (2) support of selected individuals for research, training, and other activities that may contribute to the attainment of our program goals.

Efforts in the first category have been discussed in the previous chapter under the subhead Building and Improving Institutions. Examples include support for black colleges, the development of university resources in such fields as business education and foreign-area studies, grants for independent schools of art and music, funds granted to research institutions but earmarked for research projects by individuals or teams, and grants for a range of educational institutions in the less-developed countries.

In the second category, grants have totaled an estimated $575 million since 1950—more than 10 percent of our total philanthropic expenditures. Of this amount, $350 million is accounted for by grants to other organizations that have then regranted the funds to individuals they select. Such grants included:

1. General fellowship and scholarship programs, e.g., the Upper Division Scholarships and the competitions conducted by the National Merit Scholarship Corporation and the Woodrow Wilson National Fellowship Foundation
2. Specialized fellowship programs administered by grantee organizations but designed to further Foundation program objectives (e.g., the Foreign Area Training Fellowships, administered by the Social Science Research Council, and the Graduate Fellowship Program for Black Americans, administered by the Council of Southern Universities)
3. Fellowship components of institution-building grants, a pattern used mainly in the less-developed countries

The remaining $225 million is accounted for by grants made by the Foundation directly to individual recipients whom we have selected. These grants constitute by far the largest amount of direct assistance to individuals provided by any private donor. In comparison, the Rockefeller Foundation has made grants to individuals totaling $110 million over sixty-two years. Guggenheim and Danforth, foundations known for their fellowship programs, have made grants to individuals totaling $55 million and $40 million over fifty-five and twenty-five years, respectively.

We have found our support for individuals important for the following strategic purposes:

1. *Helping to meet critical shortages of personnel with specific skills*

or competence. Such shortages are particularly acute in the less-developed countries, where they constitute major obstacles to nation-building efforts. In this connection, we have helped finance training for staffs of indigenous institutions whose development we are assisting—for example, by enabling key staff members to travel to professional meetings or to visit similar institutions. Such support has played an especially important role after the bulk of the institution-building task has been accomplished (see Case 16, p. 156).

Shortages also exist in advanced countries in fields in which rapidly changing technology or the emergence of new social issues has outstripped the supply of trained personnel. To meet such shortages, we have helped increase the number of school finance experts, lawyers familiar with ecological issues, and low-income residents trained in management of public-housing projects. Our funds often have been used as an incentive to attract talented persons into targeted fields or problem areas. This technique was used, for example, to encourage practicing engineers to teach engineering, to draw top students to foreign-area studies, and to persuade talented scientists to follow research careers in reproductive biology.

2. *Helping to strengthen individual competence, especially in new educational, scientific, or technical developments.* We have supported many programs of in-service or midcareer training, for high-level federal executives (see Case 7, p. 124), or for minority and women teachers aspiring to promotion into administrative jobs. Another approach has been through short-term grants to qualified persons who want to enhance their knowledge or competence through travel and observation, enrollment in formal training programs, or participation in conferences or seminars.

3. *Furthering individual research in fields or subjects of special Foundation interest.* We usually follow this strategy, as noted, by giving funds to autonomous organizations that then make grants to candidates they choose. However, when individual researchers are not eligible for programs conducted by other organizations, we

sometimes make grants directly. We do so especially when it seems that exploratory studies by specialists might lead to new Foundation programs or when we want an independent review of current programs.

4. *Broadening educational opportunities for young men and women who might otherwise be unable to develop their abilities.* In the 1950s, for example, we joined with Carnegie Corporation to establish the National Merit Scholarship Corporation to help promising high school students continue their education. When it was realized that hardly any blacks or other minorities were winning National Merit awards, we set up the National Achievement Scholarships ($8.1 million, 1964) exclusively for them. Later, we focused on graduate fellowships for minorities.

Among the issues that have arisen in our efforts to develop individual talents are the following:

1. There now is some indication that we (along with other donors) may have contributed to current surpluses of talent in many fields in the United States. In light of the relatively few teaching opportunities now available on college campuses, it is apparent that during the 1950s and 1960s, when we put $56 million into the Woodrow Wilson National Fellowship Foundation (our largest investment in any one fellowship program) to help young scholars prepare for university teaching careers, we failed to take into account long-term questions of supply and demand.

2. Our support of individuals may be even more susceptible to charges of favoritism and errors in judgment than our support of tax-exempt organizations. Critics inside and outside Congress charged us with an error in judgment in giving travel and study grants to eight members of the staff of Senator Robert F. Kennedy in 1968 following his assassination. The awards totaled $131,000; they reflected the Foundation's policies on individual awards; and they were for work on subjects related to the program interests of the Foundation—for example, community organization, urban economics, housing, and migratory labor. Although we regarded the recipients as able men and awarded the grants with the full

expectation that they would result in important contributions, we realized later that these grants had left us open to allegations of favoritism.

Wherever possible, we have tried to avoid such charges either by channeling support for individuals through independent grant-making organizations or by making our own awards through publicly announced competitions. In many circumstances, however, we have found that we can assist individuals effectively and expeditiously—if at all—only through direct grants awarded under more informal selection procedures. Even so, we have introduced procedural requirements and safeguards to help assure standards of fairness and quality.

3. The Internal Revenue Code, as amended by the Tax Reform Act of 1969, is more restrictive of grants to individuals than of those to organizations. In fact, the code prohibits foundations from making grants to individuals except in conformity with detailed procedures approved in advance by the Internal Revenue Service. These procedural requirements, which were probably influenced by the furor over the Kennedy staff grants, have added to our administrative burden, but they have not seriously impaired the effectiveness of programs of grants to individuals or dampened staff enthusiasm for their use.[47]

THE MULTIPLIER EFFECT

In philanthropy, the term "multiplier effect" usually means the process by which we use a grant to give an institution access to much greater funds from other sources. A multiplier effect also can be obtained by properly placing a small grant that works large

---

[47]The act also restricted support of voter registration programs and imposed a 4 percent excise tax on the annual income of foundations, reduced in 1978 to 2 percent. Other features required foundations to make annual charitable contributions at a level based on income or on a percentage of assets, whichever is higher, and to refrain from financial practices that benefit the founders, trustees, or officers. The Ford Foundation was adhering to this last group of requirements before they were legislated.

changes in a social system. We also apply the term to situations in which we enlist the resources of other foundations or of government in a common cause; in such cases, the added money is important, but equally important is the commitment of interest and expertise. Occasionally, of course, we are on the receiving end of others' efforts to produce a multiplier effect—sometimes efforts of government but more usually of other foundations (e.g., the Field Foundation enlisted our support of Kenneth Clark's Metropolitan Applied Research Center and Carnegie obtained our collaboration in the Children's Television Workshop).

Fiscal multipliers are quite familiar. A $1.4-million program-related investment matched by equivalent equity from the Corporation for Public Broadcasting and the Public Broadcasting Service triggered $38 million of long-term financing from major insurance companies to develop a satellite interconnection system; our grant of $600,000 to the Manpower Demonstration Research Corporation for development of tenant management of public housing is bringing in $20.2 million in grants from the U.S. Department of Housing and Urban Development over a three-year period; challenge grants totaling $349 million to dozens of universities and colleges in the early 1960s brought more than three times that amount in gifts and grants from other sources.

Sometimes fiscal leverage works not according to a direct proportionate matching formula, but indirectly. We may help to create local organizations and to sustain them with grants for core staff support so that they can qualify for other, much larger amounts that are available for specific projects rather than general support. Bedford-Stuyvesant Restoration Corporation, with annual core support from us of around $425,000, receives several millions of dollars every year in grants and contracts from other foundations, corporations, and federal, state, and local governments.

Indirect fiscal leverage also can be used to redirect resources that might otherwise work *against* desired social goals. Thus, the Foundation supports the Center for Community Change ($9.2 million, 1969), which monitors and reports on general revenue sharing in a widely circulated newsletter, and provides information to hundreds of local minority community development organizations on how to apply for, and if necessary lobby for, funds that might otherwise be used for restrictively expensive recreational facilities.

Efforts to enlist the resources of others most commonly involve other foundations, but they also involve professional and commercial interests and government. One of the most successful examples is the establishment of the Consultative Group on International Agricultural Research, which has multiplied funding for the international centers more than tenfold since the late 1960s, from $6 million annually from the Ford and Rockefeller foundations to $86 million in 1978 from two dozen donors, mostly governments, development banks, and multilateral organizations.

Attempts to work desirable major change on a system cannot be cited and scored in dollars, nor should they be. The Foundation subsidized the preparation and publication of Nicholas Ashford's book *Crisis in the Workplace*.[48] As the definitive contemporary work on industrial safety, this book became one of the principal policy influences on new officials in the Department of Labor's Occupational Safety and Health Administration.

Two other traditional means of producing social multiplier effects with which the Foundation is familiar are demonstration projects and civil rights litigation.

Demonstration projects are intended to move a larger system toward change by imitation. Through support of a few experiments in the early 1950s (particularly in Bay City, Michigan), we opened the educational system to the use of nonprofessional teacher aides as a regular feature in the classroom. Initial opposition by some educators faded in the face of proof that carefully selected and supervised nonprofessionals could help teachers improve instruction. The innovation developed during a period of teacher shortages, but has survived even under present teacher surpluses. In contrast, our demonstrations of instructional television essentially failed to change the pattern of instruction in American public schools (see Case 5, p. 115).

[48]Nicholas Ashford, *Crisis in the Workplace* (Cambridge, Mass.: MIT Press, 1976).

A less conclusive example was our support for alternative schools, such as the "street academies," Harlem Prep, the Federation of Community Schools in Boston, and experimental alternatives within public schools. Although several of the innovations and flexible approaches were incorporated into some public schools, the effect of the projects fell far short of what we had hoped.

Our demonstration-project support of resident theaters did result in certain changes in the field of American drama. The idea was to help develop institutions that would raise the quality of American theater and stimulate the further development of resident theater groups. Some theater companies substantially achieved high professional status. Similarly, our support of the Tamarind Lithography Workshop in California beginning in 1960, although not massive in dollar investment ($2.2 million over ten years), brought about a nationwide revival of the art of lithography, increasing both the number of workshops formed and the public's interest in and willingness to buy the work produced. Most of the printers and artists associated with the new workshops were trained in the Tamarind program, and many of them are now training others.

The much-cited Gray Areas program tested and drew attention to the free-standing local tax-exempt corporation as a means for applying government funds to locally perceived needs. As a result, this mechanism was built into the poverty programs of the 1960s. The Foundation's support of demonstration midcareer training programs for federal executives in the 1950s led to legislation that incorporated this device in U.S. Civil Service Commission procedures.

The Foundation sought to have an effect on commercial broadcasting by establishing the commercially sponsored television program "Omnibus," which ran for five years. The program cost the Foundation $3 million, and it attracted $2 million worth of advertising. Although this demonstration set a standard of quality for both commercial and public broadcasters for many years, it failed to change the commercial system, and quality programming did not become a consistent feature on the networks.

The Vera Institute has exerted considerable leverage on the criminal justice system by introducing innovations in arrest, bail, and other pretrial procedures and in sentencing. Through the supported-work program, an outgrowth of Vera experiments, the Foundation is now attempting to redirect some aspects of the welfare system in a manner far more pertinent than anything attained by a $646,000 series of studies of welfare we supported in 1969. Supported work is a national experiment to help persons such as ex-offenders, ex-addicts, and welfare-dependent mothers of young children enter the workplace and develop skills and good work habits in jobs that offer peer-group reinforcement and tolerable stress levels. Supported-work projects now are operating at fifteen sites across the country with assistance from the Department of Labor and other government agencies as well as the Foundation.

In supporting civil rights litigation and its permutations in public-interest law, we are particularly conscious that we are trying to work social change. The Foundation steers clear of selecting specific cases for litigation, but we do support the NAACP Legal Defense and Educational Fund and its Chicano, Native-American, and Puerto Rican counterparts as they litigate, in cases of their own choice, to change whole systems of employment, housing, and education. We also support such organizations as the Natural Resources Defense Council and the Environmental Defense Fund in their efforts to secure better environmental management and regulation through litigation and the development of new case law.

Still other means of seeking social change exist. Some approaches are quite direct; $2 million of support for voter education in the South over a few years helped to register hundreds of thousands of blacks, to give political power in many counties to previously disenfranchised black majorities and to help improve the social and economic climate of the region. Grants totaling $990,000 over the last ten years to the Office of Communications of the United Church of Christ supported technical assistance and litigation that threatened the licenses of radio and television stations that were discriminating against minorities in programming and employment. A number of local groups and public-interest law firms then adopted these techniques, which were continued and refined by the Office of Communications. The Federal Communications Commission thus was forced to broaden its definition of and concern for the "public interest, convenience, and necessity" that broadcasters are charged to serve. As a result, the racial policies and programming of television stations and networks have changed markedly.

Sometimes leverage can be exerted on commerce or industry to produce socially desirable results that would otherwise be unattainable. By modestly subsidizing the fees of musical performers during the recording of works of living American composers ($830,000), the Foundation helped put hundreds of works on the market through regular recording and music-publishing channels, thus helping to strengthen and diversify American musical culture.

There are limitations on efforts to bring about social change. Professional philanthropic practice usually permits work toward social change only under certain conditions. Changes must result from activities that are (1) good in themselves, such as education; (2) morally and civilly correct, such as civil rights litigation; and (3) legitimate competitors in the free market of ideas, such as demonstration projects.

One danger of encouraging substantial social change is that the effort may intrude abruptly on systems in equilibrium and thereby release the sometimes considerable forces maintaining that equilibrium. An example is the school decentralization effort in New York City, in which the Foundation assisted demonstration projects that were designed as models for other parts of the city, and, possibly, for other cities. The projects were authorized generally under state law and were sanctioned specifically by the Board of Education. But the manner in which they were conducted, along with the formulation of a controversial plan for restructuring the entire school system, contributed to the release of conflicting forces, setting unions and community groups at odds with one another. If the results of foundation-influenced social change are sufficiently spectacular, they may invite attention and reaction against the program that stimulated them and, to an extent, against foundations themselves. Voter education is a case in point. The Tax Reform Act of 1969 included explicit limitations on the use of tax-exempt funds for this purpose; it is fairly certain that these restrictions were instituted initially because congressional consciousness had been raised by the support that several foundations had given to voter registration programs in the South. A $65,000 grant made by the Foundation for a voter education and registration program confined to the black areas of Cleveland was seized on later as a "bad case" to which remedial legislative drafting was addressed. Here was an instance of our employing an insensitive means to a good end.

AN INDEPENDENT CONTRIBUTION TO PUBLIC POLICY

Our concern for public policy derives from the Foundation's roots in pluralism and pragmatism. Foundations themselves exemplify pluralism in American life. It is therefore natural that we should strive to be alert to opportunities for research and action (in ways appropriate to tax-exempt philanthropy) at the cutting edge of important social issues and problems. As noted earlier, we do so with the hope of illuminating paths to effective involvement for institutions and authorities with resources far greater than our own. But we also do so because of our belief in the advantages of a diversity of ideas and initiatives.

On the most practical level, we recognize that sooner or later, in one form or another, advances in most of the problem areas we grapple with depend on productive public policies. As we observed in 1972, when the trustees approved the establishment of a program of studies in Public Policy and Social Organization,

> Nearly all of the Foundation's current agenda of objectives and programs relate in some way to governmental activity, inactivity, or activity we may perceive as partial, inadequate, or misdirected.

In many of our enterprises, we have to look to government as a partner—a very large and sometimes a very effective partner. In other instances, we may feel that public policy is neither well formed nor well carried out, in which cases we try to support responsible critics despite the risk that they and the government may perceive each other as adversaries. We sometimes have supported institutions and individuals in an adversary role (especially as they employ litigation and other active means short of lobbying and political campaigning) when we felt the public interest would be served. But more often than not, our participation is not so dramatic and, far from being that of an adversary, may actually be invited or at least welcomed by government. In telecommunications, for example, we have responded to requests for assistance from the Federal Communications Commission by supporting research at the Rand Corporation ($200,000, 1973 and 1974), and we have tried to inform public policy on cable television at the state and local levels by establishing the Cable Television Information Center ($2.8 million, 1972).

We have come a long way in our willingness to confront public-policy issues directly. We were wary for most of the 1950s, after our few forays into policy areas (e.g., the Fund for the Republic's work on civil liberties) provoked an intense reaction in Congress. For several years thereafter, our programmatic attention to government policy was largely oblique. We made many grants to improve technical competence in government and to modernize state legislatures. We supported a range of research into such matters as metropolitan government and (through support of the National Bureau of Economic Research) growth and stability of the economy; we also maintained support of that foremost independent analyst of government, the Brookings Institution. Occasionally, we did confront an issue directly. For example, we supported a Commission on Money and Credit ($1.3 million, 1958 and 1959), which made the most searching study of the nation's financial structure in a half century. Indirectly, too, many of our actions impinged on public policy. Our support of an array of individuals and institutions associated with the Common Market implicitly supported policies directed toward European integration and Atlantic partnership. In the less-developed countries, our technical assistance from the early 1950s onward often was directly involved with public policy—for example, the Foundation's long-term support (some $4 million) for the work of the Pakistan Planning Commission.

But in the United States, it is mainly in the last dozen years or so that we have consciously and deliberately worked to affect public policy. Our activities have fallen into two main areas: (1) illumination of public policy issues, and (2) improvement of public policy processes.

Public-Policy Issues

We believe that a large private foundation has unique advantages in illuminating public-policy issues and providing a base of knowledge for their discussion. Since we serve no single interest or constituency, we can draw on a variety of views. We have developed a wide familiarity with the sources of analytical talent; we have the resources to enlist the best minds in various fields; and we are experienced in generating certain kinds of data that often are critically lacking in policy formation—information drawn directly from experience, which can often be best obtained through local demonstration projects and pilot tests in real-life settings.

To a considerable extent, the growth of the Foundation coincided with a period during which problems in many public-policy areas (e.g., national defense) became immensely more complex, while at the same time the power of modern disciplines to cast light on them improved (e.g., systems analysis). We often are the only nongovernmental funding agency available to support studies of the largest public-policy issues.

The principal means by which we have contributed to the understanding of policy issues are research and the exchange of ideas. There are, for example, policy research complements to our other efforts in a number of fields. Thus, in population, we have since 1971 supported, in collaboration with the Rockefeller Foundation, a series of awards on population and development policy issues ($3.6 million, 1968–1976). In addition, we have been an important contributor to a major center for policy analysis in population and the biomedical sciences generally, the Institute of Society, Ethics, and the Life Sciences ($293,000, 1971 and 1973). Our work in school finance over the last five years provides another example. In higher education, the record is more diffuse, but we have supported the American Council on Education and several other agencies that try, with varying degrees of success, to inform public policy.

Several public-policy centers of high professional caliber that we created or helped support enjoy high standing with the upper echelons of government. The list would include Brookings, the Urban Institute, Resources for the Future, the National Bureau of Economic Research, the domestic section of the Rand Corporation, and such specialized university centers as Wisconsin's Poverty Institute, the Harvard-MIT Joint Center for Urban Studies, George Washington University's Center for Manpower Policy Studies, and the criminal-justice centers at the University of Chicago and Harvard. Internationally, the Foundation has supported high-quality public-policy research and training at a number of institutions, including the Economic Research Centre (Ireland), the Dalhousie Governmental Studies Program (Canada), the Center for Economic Development and Administration (Nepal), the Institute of Economic Growth (India), the Foundation for Higher Education and Development (Colombia), the Center for Regional Development and Planning (Brazil), and the National Institute of Social and Economic Research (Nigeria).

In some cases, our support has been joined with a government's support. For example, our funds help the Urban Institute to maintain its independence, although it could not survive without heavy government support.

Our record of supporting research that contributes to policy on international relations is long and in some instances distinguished. It extends from our assistance to the International Institute for Strategic Studies, an independent center for research, information, and debate on problems of security, conflict, and arms control, to Brookings's foreign policy analyses and to the current series of grants for research on arms control, to say nothing of the mass of research supported under the International Training and Research program.

In several other fields—housing, day care, manpower, and drug abuse, to name a few—various grantees produce research that commands respectful attention from diverse parties to public-policy formation.

We have been active in ventilating policy issues as well as in underwriting research on them. On the premise that right-minded governmental policies are unlikely to succeed without a right-minded citizenry, we have supported public information efforts ranging from organized media campaigns (e.g., on housing discrimination) to attempts at long-term modifications of educational curricula (e.g., school programs on the Bill of Rights, the environment, foreign policy, and so on). One difficulty here is not only that so many competing interests wish to use the schools and the media to advance a cause but also that so little is reliably known about the relation between education and attitudes. Nonetheless, we support many institutions devoted substantially, if not entirely, to policy discussion and information dissemination—for example, the Overseas Development Council, the National Committee for Citizens in Education, the Day Care and Child Development Council, the National Committee Against Discrimination in Housing, and the Southern Regional Council. We have helped place particular issues on the agendas of such prominent forums as the American Assembly and the Aspen Institute. And we have assisted selected magazines and scholarly journals chartered to undertake policy discussion: *Change, Daedalus, The Public Interest,* and *Corrections.*

To help ensure high-quality journalistic coverage of policy issues, we have supported several efforts (often in collaboration with newspaper and broadcasting organizations) to provide reporters and editors with the time and means to improve their analytical skills. Such programs have ranged from the American Political Science Association's journalist internships with congressmen in the 1950s to a recent series of midcareer fellowships that enable journalists to concentrate for several months on such important public-policy areas as unemployment and arms control.

Public-Policy Processes

Enlightened public policy depends not only on knowledge and understanding but also on accessibility to the processes by which policies are formed and on equity in decision-making. We have therefore sought:

- to improve the competence of public policymakers
- to support private-sector activities to influence the direction of public policy
- to ensure the fairness and openness of public processes
- to collaborate with decision makers and others in government in the pursuit of shared objectives

As for our desire to raise the caliber of policymakers, the current program in support of graduate education for public service (see Case 2, p. 97), is the latest in a long chain of efforts to attract talented men and women to public life and policy analysis and to provide appropriate training for them and for incumbent policymakers. In the 1950s, we granted $2 million to the National Center for Education in Politics (formerly the Citizenship Clearing House) to involve college students in community affairs and in political-party activities. To improve scholarly research on the legislative process and to afford congressional policymakers direct and continuing access to the academic world, we supported internships in Congress for faculty members ($1.6 million over ten years to the American Political Science Association). Similar internships were supported at the state legislative level, as were internships for some 200 graduate students in the offices of governors, mayors, and other state and local administrators. As noted earlier, along with other efforts to improve the competence of government decision-makers, we supported Career Education Awards to enable young federal executives to spend a year in graduate study at major universities. There was at least a stated public-policy rationale in our support of leading law schools in the 1950s

> to enrich legal education as a preparation for public responsibility, to stimulate legal research on contemporary public problems . . . and to assist efforts to make the law a more effective instrument of democratic government.

As this series of grants to law schools drew to a close, we judged the results to range from good to indifferent. In some areas, we have institutionalized efforts to upgrade policymakers; for example, we helped create the Institute for Educational Leadership ($5.8 million since 1971), which operates state and national internships for young educational policymakers and seminars for officials from federal and state education agencies.

In the last dozen years, we have added to our public-policy efforts the dimension of minority participation in policymaking. Our support of voting rights has probably been the single most effective effort in this direction, but we also have helped train minority elected officials, recruit blacks and others to professions such as planning in which they might rise to policymaking levels, and establish minority-run centers of policy analysis, such as the Black Economic Research Center and the Joint Center for Political Studies.

Our present support of graduate public-policy programs is not so much a case of coming full circle as it is one of capitalizing on radically changed circumstances. New university-based programs of advanced training and research on public policymaking and management emerged without us. In relatively short order, they have achieved status within leading universities. We have come to their aid because they satisfy our long-standing, but also long-frustrated, interest in helping establish first-class programs of advanced, professional training for young people aiming at public service.

Among the more immediate ways of affecting public policy, as we have said earlier, is litigation. In civil rights law and in public-interest law, we have supported organizations that have applied legal skills to a vast array of public-policy questions in education, employment, political participation, and environmental protection. A debate now is under way about the extent to which litigation should be a moving force in public policy. As evidenced by our increased emphasis on mediation and conflict resolution, we too believe it is time to take stock, but not to come to a halt.

In addition to helping lawyers, we more recently have assisted organizations of publicly oriented economists, accountants, and tax analysts who are trying to bring about greater equity in public-policymaking processes.

We have extensively supported organizations that use other tools to improve public policies or to ensure that well-conceived policies already in place are in fact applied faithfully and diligently. Prominent examples would include the Center for National Policy Review (Catholic University), the Southern Regional Council, the United Church of Christ Office of Communications, and the Center for Community Change. The methods of these organizations include monitoring and evaluation of government programs, representations to the responsible agencies and individuals, and technical assistance to local organizations. Our support of the legislative reapportionment efforts of the National Municipal League in the early 1960s ($994,000) illustrates that we have sometimes been able to help hasten the implementation of public policy. Data provided by the National Municipal League are credited with having helped the Supreme Court accelerate its follow-up to the "one man-one vote" decision *(Baker* v. *Carr)* with a definitive ruling on reapportionment.

Finally, we have participated in the public-policy process through direct links with government. One such link, in this field, as in others, is the experiment or demonstration program that serves as a model for government action. For example, our experience in the inner city, in the arts, and in preschool education provided important evidence for major federal legislation in these fields in the 1960s. Links also are forged through informal contact between Foundation staff members and government agencies in their fields; our support of research and experiments on the quality of working life, for example, is serving as an external legitimizing device for what a government agency (e.g., the Economic Development Administration) may already want to do or eventually may decide to do after associating with our staff. We also have been asked by congressional committees to submit information and to testify in areas of our experience. In public broadcasting, a lion's share of the credit for the major policy change that uncorked direct federal support should go to the Johnson administration, which, when approached by public broadcasting officials about a special private commission on the subject, said that such a commission would have its blessing. The establishment of the Corporation for Public Broadcasting (CPB) in 1967 followed the Carnegie Commission report. By sharing our long experience in the field with CPB, we played an indirect role in the way federal policy subsequently developed, particularly in support of the concept of strong program production centers. As the policy evolved, we used our funds strategically to ensure the independence and integrity of the public broadcasting enterprise as it shifted to federal support.

In other policy-related cases, we have collaborated directly with government. Currently, our work in tenant management, neighborhood housing preservation, and supported work for the severely disadvantaged—all in partnership with government—is providing experience that has affected policies and that has potential for more changes.

We are not uniformly successful, to say the least, in trying to direct public policy into what we consider the best channels, but our appetite for tough issues has grown nonetheless.

Most of the Foundation's regular units continue to encourage possible public-policy remedies for problems in their spheres of interest—population, nuclear energy studies, arms control, and educational finance, to cite a few. And since it was established five years ago, the Foundation-wide Committee on Public Policy and Social Organization has underwritten studies of problems of fundamental importance—the distribution of wealth and social status; the changing conditions of American social institutions and societal values; the ramifications of Watergate; the uncertain relations between theories of economics and economic policy outcomes; issues concerning Vietnam veterans, deserters, and draft evaders; and the problems and interrelations that underlie the judicial system.

In many crucial areas of the nation's domestic life, the level of public debate is low and the pace of public policymaking is sluggish, while at the same time the tolerance for ineffective legal and governmental institutions has worn thin. In these circumstances, we are likely to continue being receptive to requests for support of constructive, independent contributions to public policy.

Case Studies

CASE 1. REPRODUCTIVE BIOLOGY:
         LEADERSHIP/PARTNERSHIP

Although the Foundation did not mount a major effort in population until 1959, we began to support work on the subject in
1952 through our Behavioral Sciences program. Our support was
initiated because certain trustees were strongly interested in
Planned Parenthood.

Most of our assistance the first few years (averaging $300,000
annually from 1952 through 1958) went to the Population Council.
At the time we specifically excluded work in reproductive biology.
Our public posture was that the Foundation eschewed any support
of medical research; an additional constraint was our feeling that
from a public-relations viewpoint, contraceptive research was too
controversial.[49]

Altogether, our population effort has totaled some $200 mil-
lion. Half of this has supported research in the reproductive

[49]In 1952 the world was not generally aware of the existence of a population explosion in the developing nations, stemming from sharp reductions in the death rate.

93

sciences and the development of contraceptives.[50] The biomedical work is discussed here.

Our objective has been to accelerate the development of better methods of birth control. This approach is analogous to the Foundation's support of agricultural research institutes to develop improved strains of grain and other agricultural products.

It is a commonplace that people need to be motivated to control their family size. The Foundation is encouraging the quest for better contraception in the awareness that at any given level of motivation, the better the acceptability, safety, and reliability of a contraceptive, the more it is likely to be used. We have supported a wide range of programs from training and research in fundamental reproductive biology to contraceptive product development.

The fundamental research has been conducted primarily by research groups in medical schools in the United States, Europe, and other industrialized countries. In the developing world we support both centers that conduct research of international quality and less sophisticated laboratories and clinics that are developing expertise in local evaluation of contraceptives that may have been developed elsewhere. The Foundation has also supported a number of research institutes that conduct both fundamental and applied research, such as the Population Council, the Worcester Foundation, and the Salk Institute. Not only have we provided supplementary support to existing research groups, but large Foundation grants have helped establish major new centers (e.g., those at the University of Southern California, Harvard, Columbia, and the University of Pennsylvania).

We have also assisted in institutional innovation. Product development is usually left to private industry. But private firms have found that development costs in preparing contraceptives specially suited to the developing world (i.e., those that are inexpensive and require infrequent repeat dosage) are too great in relation to expected profit. Thus, the Foundation has supported contraceptive

[50]The rest has been devoted to social science research relevant to population policy and the improved management and evaluation of population programs.

product development in the public sector. These practical research efforts, also supported by national governments, include the World Health Organization's Expanded Programme in Human Reproduction and the Population Council's International Committee for Contraceptive Research. In collaboration with nonprofit research laboratories and private industry, the Foundation has helped develop patent agreements that protect the public interest but also preserve adequate incentives for private industry to invest in product development and distribution.

The Foundation has also encouraged able young people to enter research in the reproductive sciences by financing graduate and postdoctoral fellowships. An estimated five hundred individuals have received one or more years of research training through Foundation funds. Reproductive research is no longer a low-status field for medical scientists, since research interests tend to follow paths marked out by funds.

As to results, Foundation funding has surely contributed to an explosion of new fundamental knowledge in reproduction, although *the* device—the "miracle rice" of birth control—has not been invented.

The oral contraceptive had been developed prior to the Foundation's entry into the field. With small-scale philanthropic support, scientists at the Worcester Foundation had taken advantage of the advances in steroid chemistry pursued by private drug companies for other purposes. The Population Council, substantially financed by the Foundation, acted as entrepreneur in the development of modern intrauterine contraception, first the plastic loop and, more recently, the copper T. A small Foundation grant to Antonio Scommegna at the Michael Reese Hospital in Chicago resulted in the development of an intrauterine device that provides a low dose of the hormone progestin directly to the uterus; it is being brought to market under a patent agreement with a private company. The most exciting new contraceptive lead (among some dozen now undergoing clinical trials) is a contraceptive vaccine. The initial clinical applications of the vaccine were made by Pran Talwar of the All-India Institute of Medical Sciences, a Foundation grantee. However, worldwide clinical trials of the vaccine are still to be completed, and until they are we will not know whether it is safe enough for general use.

Another result of the Foundation's involvement in reproductive research has been heightened attention to questions of ethics in human experimentation in clinics outside the United States.

Since we entered the field of reproductive biology we have paid careful attention to the interaction of our role with that of other funding sources. For nearly a decade, we were the principal private source of support, with our grants outstripping even the amounts given by domestic or foreign government agencies.[51] Foundation officers and staff have consulted with other private and public funding sources frequently and have written and testified about the state of the field. We have encouraged other agencies, including AID, to increase their support; AID is now the largest source of population program funds. Two Foundation staff members, Oscar Harkavy and Anna L. Southam, developed an estimate of an optimum level of support for the field—$150 million a year as of 1967—which received widespread circulation among government policymakers. Contained in a consultant's report to the Department of Health, Education and Welfare, it had a direct effect on the subsequent increase in government funding for reproductive research. Our latest effort to encourage others to increase their support is a major review of the field, *Reproduction and Human Welfare: A Challenge to Research*, which was published in 1976.

The period from 1965 to 1973 saw substantial increases in support from all sources (and particularly from the National Institutes of Health), from $3.7 million to $117.4 million. The Foundation's contribution declined from 16 percent of the total to 9 percent, although in absolute terms our contribution more than doubled. Since 1973, however, all funding for reproductive sciences and contraceptive development has declined. Reproductive research is

---

[51]In 1959, when the first Foundation grant in reproductive biology was made ($700,000 to the Population Council), *Fortune* magazine estimated that only $800,000 was provided by all funding agencies in support of the reproductive sciences.

much better funded in the United States than in other industrial countries, where medical research councils provide relatively insignificant sums for support of the field. But even in the United States, the growth of research capacity has outstripped available support. Thus, the expectations of the research community are being substantially frustrated. It seems likely that talent will flow away from reproductive biology to such higher-priority areas as cancer research, which now receives one-third of the NIH budget. Thus, while the Foundation is no longer a major source of support, its funds continue to be in urgent demand.

CASE 2. UNIVERSITIES: NEW AGENDAS

The Foundation has worked with universities to meet a variety of objectives, some primarily formulated by the universities, others by us. Following are brief descriptions of five of the Foundation's university programs. They range in scope and detail from International Studies, the largest and most varied, to the Public Policy program, the smallest and most selective. The Graduate Education program was designed mainly to affect the ways graduate schools operate. In the Business Education program the Foundation probably made its most concentrated effort to develop a whole new body of knowledge and to encourage a redirection of the professional schools in which that knowledge emerged.

Graduate Education

In 1967 the Foundation launched a major experimental seven-year program to improve the efficiency of graduate education in the humanities and social sciences. The overall cost was $41.5 million. The main objective was to establish patterns of full-time study and apprentice teaching leading to a Ph.D. in approximately four years. Other aims were to reduce attrition among graduate students and to provide systematic teaching experience as a regular component of doctoral study.

Ten leading schools received grants ranging from $4 million to $4.4 million, to be used for fellowships and teaching assistantships for participating students. The institutions selected, which were then awarding about 30 percent of all Ph.D.'s in the humanities and social sciences, were California (Berkeley), Chicago, Cornell, Harvard, Michigan, Pennsylvania, Princeton, Stanford, Wisconsin, and Yale. Foundation funds were matched, roughly four-to-one, by the universities' own resources and other fellowship funds, thus adding another $160 million to the program. It was anticipated that some 10,500 students would be covered by the program during the period 1967–1974.

External factors complicated the effort almost from the beginning. The federal government sharply cut back its graduate fellowships, thus eroding the student financial support on which the program was based. During the early years, the war in Vietnam created problems for students subject to the draft, tending to interrupt or prolong graduate study. During the final years of the program the "Ph.D. glut," a general economic recession, and projection of declining undergraduate enrollment created concern about employment possibilities.

Although the participating universities shared common objectives, they allocated the funds in different ways according to local needs and circumstances. It was therefore difficult to generate a uniform set of data on which to base judgments about overall results. Moreover, the general rules governing the use of Foundation funds were not always clearly understood or observed at the departmental level.

A full-scale evaluation of the program was conducted at the end of the grant period. Little or no improvement in the median duration of graduate study in the humanities and social sciences was found in the ten universities or in the country at large. The four-year norm remained an elusive objective. By 1974 no field, with the exception of economics, showed a median time for completion of the doctorate below seven years, and some were more than eight years. Through better monitoring of students and through the eliminating of obsolete course requirements, the pre-dissertation stage has been shortened. The dissertation remains the main obstacle to rapid completion of the degree, and financial support does not appear to be sufficient to overcome this obstacle. The program appears to have had little effect on attrition; factors other than the availability of fellowship funding appear to be the dominant element. Minor gains were made in providing teaching experience as an integral part of doctoral training.

On the whole, this large program did not have a significant effect on the ways major universities conduct their Ph.D. training programs.

Urban Research and Training

Foundation grants to universities for work on urban affairs, totaling some $36 million, have had two objectives: (1) to encourage closer contact between university scholars and government decision-makers in order that research results could be applied to urban ills; and (2) to promote research and graduate study on a wide range of urban problems by scholars from a variety of disciplines.

We first seriously entered the field at the end of the 1950s, funding (with $4.5 million) a series of "urban extension" experiments to encourage state universities (Rutgers, Delaware, Wisconsin, Purdue, Illinois, Missouri, Berkeley, and Oklahoma) to replicate the experience of the nineteenth century with agricultural extension agents. The experiment had mixed results. In several cases—where projects were well funded, had capable leadership, and were located in cities of moderate size with moderate difficulties—the experiment seemed to work well. The urban extension agents were well received and left a lasting imprint, particularly in the ghetto communities where they operated. In other cases, the experiments never got off the ground, and today there is scarcely a trace of the Foundation's effort. Nor has the urban extension idea swept the country or attracted the kind of university commitment and government funding that many of its adherents hoped it would.

Also in the late 1950s, we began an eight-year effort to turn the attention of the economics profession toward the city. The program, administered by Resources for the Future's Committee on Urban Economics, spent about $1.25 million trying to encourage professional economists to focus more effort on what was happening in the nation's cities. The program produced about forty Ph.D.'s, helped to establish half a dozen urban research centers, and promoted a number of research projects in what was, at the time, virtually an unknown field. The money was well spent. Today, most graduate programs in economics offer urban and regional economics courses, and in the largest universities Ph.D. degrees with this specialization are popular.

Another wave of grants came in the late 1960s and early 1970s, with about $30 million being distributed to some dozen universities to help them turn their attention to the urban scene. This effort reflected our conviction that universities were contributing distressingly little to an understanding of the "urban crisis" and that in many cases they were either targets of rioters or contributed directly to the widespread turmoil. Most grants supported research programs at newly created urban studies centers. In addition, a dozen professorships in urban studies were endowed at Harvard, MIT, Columbia, and Chicago, and a wide variety of specific research projects were funded. This multimillion-dollar research expenditure produced considerable discipline-oriented research of merit, but its output in terms of research applicable to urban policy was negligible. The new endowed chairs probably encouraged several scholars to concentrate their efforts more intensively on urban problems than they might otherwise have done. In addition, our funds helped a substantial number of graduate students to do dissertations on urban projects, and many journal articles and books were published. It is difficult, however, to identify breakthroughs in our understanding of how cities operate, what makes them grow or wither, what produces harmony or conflict, or how successful government, greater citizen participation, and efficient delivery of services can be attained.

University efforts to be of direct service to governmental and private decision-makers present an even bleaker picture. It remains questionable whether any progress has been made toward developing productive working relations between the academy and urban leaders.

The urban unrest of the late 1960s stimulated other funding sources to enter this field. Universities themselves made modest commitments to urban studies, particularly through the establishment of urban research centers and the introduction of new courses, and often new degrees, with an urban focus. The federal government funded numerous studies of city problems and made a limited number of graduate fellowships available through the Department of Housing and Urban Development.

The Foundation's departure from this field was hastened by our budget contractions of 1974 and 1975. As with many subjects of widespread concern, other funding sources have also reduced their contributions, and research and educational programs that are clearly urban in focus have fallen on hard times. There is, however, an obvious lasting impact in the many research centers established during this period, with and without our help, and in the curriculum changes that give greater attention to the analytical and policy problems of our cities.

Public-Policy Programs

For some years the Foundation had a broad, if loosely defined, interest in helping universities to prepare young people for public service. We sporadically have given grants to assist graduate training and research activities in programs of public administration, public and international affairs (as distinct from foreign area centers, as discussed later), or urban affairs. Only with the creation of the Committee on Public Policy and Social Organization in March 1972, however, was a part of the Foundation given continuing responsibility for systematic attention to "helping establish or strengthen first-class programs of advanced professional training for young people aiming at public service."

The committee's principal approach has been a series of general-support grants, totaling $2,550,000, to eight graduate-level institutions.[52] In selecting the centers it would support, the committee excluded from consideration both conventional social science departments organized by discipline and traditional schools of public administration, and gave preference to interdisciplinary, professionally oriented public-policy programs. The committee favored programs that were already under way but still new enough to be flexible and experimental. It also looked for programs in which the leadership was vigorous, imaginative, and effective, the backing of the central administration firm, and the possibility of sustained funding real. The committee did not believe that there was any single "right" mold in which all programs should be cast. Rather, it sought to contribute to diversity of experience by assisting a variety of models with some common elements. The funds have been used primarily for curriculum development, fellowships for graduate students, "clinical" programs for students, salaries for new faculty appointees, and research awards to faculty.

Progress in the programs has been uneven, and important questions remain about their organization, their place within the university, the content of their curricula, and the career patterns of the graduates. Nevertheless, the apparent success of the programs to date is noteworthy, as indicated by the intellectual liveliness of the faculties, the seriousness of the work in curriculum development, the high motivation and brightness of the students, and the healthy demand in public agencies for the graduates. The programs are training a new breed of policy analysts and public managers, while helping to break down rigid divisions among disciplines and schools within universities. The new programs are attracting stronger students and faculty members than the older public-administration schools and are finding interesting new ways to

[52]The Graduate School of Public Policy at Berkeley, the School of Urban and Public Affairs at Carnegie-Mellon, the John F. Kennedy School of Government at Harvard, the Institute of Public Policy Studies at Michigan, the Graduate School of Business at Stanford, the Lyndon B. Johnson School of Public Affairs at Texas, the Institute of Policy Sciences and Public Affairs at Duke, and the Graduate Institute of the Rand Corporation.

analyze social problems and to suggest solutions through public policy.

The field of policy analysis is still in its formative stages and requires continued support. The Committee on Public Policy and Social Organization has therefore invited each of the initial grantees to submit proposals for terminal grants, totaling approximately $1 million; it also is exploring possibilities for making similar institutional-support grants to one or two additional schools. In addition, the committee may assist innovative developments within the field by supporting cooperative and competitive activities among the programs.

International Studies

The emergence of the United States as a world power after World War II underscored the national need for expertise about "non-Western" societies—that is, nearly all countries beyond the boundaries of Western Europe and North America. It was evident to us that knowledge about foreign areas could be best developed by supporting training and research within universities.

Some major universities harbored nuclei of scholars who studied China or Russia or India or Latin America, generally from literary or historical points of view. There were also a few language and area experts trained to carry on activities required by the war effort. But many more experts were needed. The study of Africa, Eastern Europe, and Southeast Asia had barely begun,[53] and among social scientists only historians and anthropologists had been involved in foreign studies.

Our strategy was to move first to support the training of individuals and then to try to improve institutions. We aimed to support both the development of experts through training and the development of knowledge through research. Ideally, these objectives coincide when advanced students prepare dissertations. The

[53]Not until the late 1960s was it argued that special encouragement had to be given to social scientists with an interest in Western Europe if that field of interest was to compete within universities with "non-Western" concerns.

Foreign Area Fellowship Program, which made awards to American and Canadian students for graduate training, including overseas research, began in 1952 and continues in substance to the present. It has been judged very effective. Funds committed for individual awards have totaled some $45 million. The awards have carried considerable prestige, and a high proportion of today's foreign-area scholars are alumni of the program.

Our support of individual postdoctoral research, like our support of graduate students, has been carried out through awards administered by committees of scholars jointly appointed by the Social Science Research Council and the American Council of Learned Societies. There is general satisfaction with the high quality of the research that has emerged, but some concern about coverage among the scholarly disciplines.

The second major component of the International Studies program was support to universities, specifically to area studies centers and to centers or schools dealing with law, international affairs, comparative international studies, or comparative education. These grants totaled some $190 million. Beginning in the 1960s, multimillion-dollar grants went to such universities as Harvard, Chicago, Columbia, California (Berkeley), UCLA, Stanford, Cornell, Michigan, MIT, Indiana, and Yale, and smaller grants to universities like Princeton and Pennsylvania. We also made grants to universities that were outstanding in their geographical regions, like Duke or the University of Denver or Washington University, or that were noted for rendering special service to developing countries, like Michigan State, Pittsburgh, or Syracuse. Our objectives were to ensure the development of high-quality efforts and to "broaden the resource base" for international studies. The grant funds were put to a wide range of uses: faculty salaries, graduate fellowships, faculty research, library acquisitions and specialized staff, travel, lectures, secretarial assistance, publication costs, and administrative expenses. Some grants to major private universities included endowment of professorial chairs and, occasionally, funds for building costs. At all the universities, our funds were designed to build new organizational structures to compete with established ones. By commanding outside financial resources, the new centers acquired the capacity to fund research and influence appointments. In most instances, at the Foundation's urging, a university-wide administrative unit was established to deal with the institution's international interests.

Did massive infusions of money and new organizational forms produce long-lasting "internationalization" of universities? The answer is, for the most part, positive. In all the universities that received funding, many more internationally oriented social scientists are doing research on non-Western areas and teaching graduate and undergraduate students about those areas. Expansion of international concerns owed a great deal to our funding, although there were, in a period of general growth at universities, many other sources of support. Even in the current period of retrenchment, international studies in universities, while no less vulnerable than other fields to budget and staff cuts, remain well established.

In the late 1960s, university administrators feared that the termination of our funding of international studies would have devastating consequences for their programs, and they persuaded the Foundation to provide "transitional" funds ($9 million) to flatten the curve of declining support. It is still too early to judge what these funds may have accomplished; international studies show a tenacious survival in many places and some administrators may have been too panicky, but making the reduction of support more gradual has probably helped many interests survive. In 1975, a series of "tie-off" grants to nine centers explicitly terminated the long process of institution-building.

Qualitatively, there were few big surprises in our effort to internationalize the universities: those institutions with the best general reputations developed the best international studies programs. Yet, grants to second-ranked universities were generally well used. If our exclusive objective had been academic excellence, and if we had had less money to spend, we would have done well to concentrate our support in the major research universities; but funds were relatively abundant and the pursuit of diverse objectives possible.

Business Education

In 1957 the Ford Foundation undertook a major effort to strengthen business education in the United States. Between 1957 and 1965 grants totaling $46.3 million were made under the program. This new effort emerged from our already established Program in Economic Development and Administration, which was concerned with research, training, and the dissemination of knowledge in economics and business administration. As this work progressed, it became increasingly clear that a special effort in the field of business administration was needed.

Schools of business were established in American colleges and universities shortly after the turn of the century and in the ensuing decades grew phenomenally. By the 1950s one out of seven of all degrees awarded was in business administration, a proportion exceeded only by degrees in education. At the same time business schools, with a few notable exceptions, were held in low esteem in the academic community and to some extent in the business world as well. For the most part the schools were characterized by narrow vocational curricula, low standards of admission, and less than scholarly students and faculties.

We directed attention to these problems through the following activities:

- A fellowship program for doctoral students (the first of its kind in the field) to increase the supply and improve the quality of teachers
- Faculty study and research fellowships designed to encourage updating of knowledge and skills and provide increased opportunities for basic research
- Regional workshops and seminars to inform faculties about the newest concepts and research findings and about their application to business studies

- Reports, studies, and conferences on curricula to encourage the development of new courses and teaching methods[54]
- Support for preparation and dissemination of teaching materials
- Support for research on business by faculty members in related social sciences and other disciplines
- General support to the major institutions in the field for the development of graduate programs

Many of the new approaches were pioneered by the relatively young Graduate School of Industrial Administration at Carnegie-Mellon University, but Harvard, Stanford, and Chicago also played strong roles.

These activities have had a profound effect on the quality and prestige of American business schools. Indeed, the changes were widely referred to at the time as a revolution in business education. The Foundation's efforts were successful in (1) shifting the emphasis of collegiate education for business from vocational undergraduate programs to graduate professional programs; (2) broadening, liberalizing, and generally strengthening curricula through the incorporation of social science concepts and rigorous quantitative methods; (3) raising the scholarly level of business faculty members to full equality with their counterparts in other disciplines; and (4) developing high-quality interdisciplinary schools within a handful of universities. One of the few criticisms of the program is that its doctoral studies and research activity may have become too theoretical and esoteric.

With its objectives largely achieved, the Foundation terminated the business education program in 1965, phasing out its activities gradually over a two- to three-year period. From a new position of strength the schools continued to grow and flourish. Their graduates are in high demand, their faculties are able to compete successfully for research grants and contracts, and in-

---

[54]The most notable study was the widely disseminated volume entitled *Higher Education for Business*, by Professors Robert A. Gordon of Berkeley and James E. Howell of Stanford (New York: Columbia University Press, 1959).

creased support from the business community has been forthcoming.

CASE 3.   LEGAL DEFENSE FOR THE POOR: A RUNNING START

By 1963, when the Supreme Court decreed in *Gideon* v. *Wainwright* that defendants, poor or rich, must be provided counsel, the Foundation had already begun to work on the expansion and improvement of publicly supported defense of the indigent accused. Three months before the court's decision, the trustees appropriated $2.4 million for the newly formed National Defender Project (NDP) of the National Legal Aid and Defender Association, which was the culmination of a Foundation-supported pilot project. With Foundation support eventually totaling $6.3 million, the NDP was responsible for establishing throughout the United States model programs for publicly supported defender services to meet the requirements of *Gideon* and of a subsequent decision that closed its loopholes. Although public-defender services are still far from what they ought to be, the NDP accelerated their development by many years. Furthermore, the project sowed the seeds for the legal-services program that became a major feature of the federal "war against poverty" in the 1960s.

Support of legal services for the indigent accused marked the Foundation's first direct intervention in the justice system, although not its first venture into legal affairs. In the 1950s the Foundation had spent $8.7 million in what later observers termed a naive "leap of faith," an attempt to direct the talent of the legal profession toward public service by providing graduate fellowships and professorships at prominent law schools (Harvard, Columbia, Yale, NYU, Stanford, Michigan, University of California) for the training of law teachers to educate students in "public affairs." By all accounts, the funds were absorbed without any discernible effect on the quality of lawyers entering politics and government.

We had also supported some research through the Behavioral Sciences program and through grants of $570,000 to the American Bar Foundation in the mid-1950s. After considerable prodding by the Foundation, the ABF produced five volumes—on detection, arrest, prosecution, conviction, and sentencing—from 1965 through 1970. The research had little effect on the criminal justice system, but it did constitute the first comprehensive examination of the subject since the Wickersham Commission in 1931.

At the time the Foundation entered the criminal defense field, only one state (California) had an adequate public-defender program. Most of the 100 local defender offices in sixteen states had only one lawyer working part time with inadequate funds. None could provide assistance for all accused indigents, many would not accept murder or other capital cases, and few could undertake appeals. The private sector was even less effective. Legal aid societies were (and still are in many places) a weak, or even grudging, bow by the organized bar to the notion that legal services should be available even to those who cannot afford them. Legal aid was underfunded and provided little incentive to young or older members of the bar to participate. Services in criminal cases were even weaker than on the civil side. The National Legal Aid Association, to which, incidentally, the Foundation had granted $120,000 for general support in 1953, did not include the word "defender" in its title until 1959. Less than $5 million a year was being spent on legal aid throughout the country.

Although two trustees of the Foundation were interested in helping law schools just below the top layer, neither the staff nor the trustees had shown any interest in the Foundation's taking a direct role in improving the criminal justice system. That changed with the arrival on the staff of William Pincus, a former federal official who came to the Foundation to conduct programs in public administration. He was a lawyer (though he had not practiced criminal law), and his interests here soon turned to criminal justice. In effect he backed the Foundation into the field by picking up the threads of interest in helping law schools produce more "publicly responsible" lawyers. He won support in the organized bar and among law schools for a national series of experiments exposing law students to "social practice" through internships with welfare agencies, police departments, prosecutors' offices, lower courts, and civil rights groups. The program was institutionalized in 1959 in the National Council on Legal Clinics, assisted with Foundation grants totaling $1,750,000.[55]

Among the places where students served internships were defender offices and legal aid societies. The Foundation followed up this program by conducting, with the help of a consultant who had been a prosecutor, a national survey of defender offices. With the evidence of the sorry state of public defense in hand, the staff won trustee approval for the National Defender Project.

The NDP was a great success, not only because of its coincidence with the Supreme Court ruling, but also because of its choice of director, a former U.S. Army Judge Advocate who was experienced in dealing with both political figures and chief judges of state courts throughout the country. The *Gideon* decision raised enormous problems for jurisdictions throughout the country. To cope with them the National Defender Project was able to provide technical assistance and modest start-up matching funds to help answer such questions as, Where are experienced trial lawyers and supporting staff to be found? and, How should compensation for lawyers handling cases for criminally accused indigents be obtained? The NDP worked with state and local authorities, law schools, and federal agencies. Within the next few years Congress passed the Criminal Justice Act, which established standards of representation in federal courts and compensation for counsel called on to defend poor citizens; following the act more than half the states reformed procedures bearing on the appointment and compensation of lawyers defending impoverished clients.

Funds from the NDP were used early on to finance the criminal defense part of the general legal-services offices established in Foundation-supported antipoverty programs in New Haven,

[55]The council was the forerunner of the Council on Legal Education for Professional Responsibility, for which the Foundation has granted $10.9 million.

Philadelphia, and Washington. They were the forerunners of the legal-services program originally run by the U.S. Office of Economic Opportunity and currently administered by the National Legal Services Corporation.

On two main grounds, then, the defender project was significant: (1) It marked one of the first instances, outside the educational field, of the Foundation's commitment of substantial funds to an important social objective through direct intervention; and (2) it provided American society with a head start on remedying a severe social inequity.

CASE 4.   ARMS CONTROL: THE CONTINUING URGENCY

World peace has been a primary concern of the Foundation from the beginning. The 1950 trustee report called for work toward "the mitigation of tensions which now threaten world peace" and "the development among the peoples of the world of the understanding and conditions essential to permanent peace." The emphasis on peace was natural considering the times. The memory of World War II was fresh, and even more disastrous conflict with the USSR or China seemed increasingly possible.

We have taken a variety of approaches to the search for peace. We have tried to strengthen international institutions, including the United Nations.[56] World peace through law was the ultimate target of a long-term program of assistance in international legal studies ($18.6 million).[57] Individual grants were made to encourage the exploration of new international structures. A range of program activities in citizen education for world affairs, international training and research in colleges and universities, and even overseas development were predicated in large part on the assumption that

[56]Altogether, we have granted $22.4 million to the U.N. and U.N.-related institutions, $20.7 million of which has been devoted to the U.N. Library, the U.N. School, and the U.N. Development Corporation.
[57]See *Architects of Order* (New York: Ford Foundation, 1959).

they would help to bring peace, stability, and improvement in the conduct of human affairs on a global scale.

Projects concerned directly with military strategy, arms, and the highly technical aspects of conflict and its limitation are another part of a general approach to the problem of peace. In the 1950s and early 1960s modest grants were given for research on nuclear and radiation-related topics. Larger grants—in the $200,000 to $500,000 range (to Harvard, Columbia, MIT, and the Institute for Defense Analysis, for example)—went for studies of defense policy. Support also went to individuals for studies of the specific issue of arms control and disarmament. Various conference series (e.g., Pugwash, Dartmouth) were assisted in bringing together experts from the West and the Soviet bloc to explore opportunities for specific implementation of new arms-related concepts.

Perhaps the most important single set of grants in the security field was for the establishment and subsequent nurture of the International Institute for Strategic Studies (IISS), $1.4 million since 1959.

In general these grants have been evaluated very positively. In particular the Foundation can point to solid accomplishment in its efforts to encourage fresh conceptual work in arms control and international security. Such seminal studies as Henry Kissinger's *Nuclear Weapons and Foreign Policy*[58] and *The Necessity for Choice*,[59] Thomas Schelling and Morton Halperin's *Strategy and Arms Control*,[60] and John Maddox and Leonard Beaton's book *The Spread of Nuclear Weapons*[61] have been produced under our grants. On the issue of coming to terms with modern weapons, we sponsored a rather utopian study of universal disarmament written under the

---

[58]Henry Kissinger, *Nuclear Weapons and Foreign Policy* (New York: Council on Foreign Relations, 1957).

[59]Henry Kissinger, *The Necessity for Choice* (New York: Harper, 1961).

[60]Thomas Schelling and Morton Halperin, *Strategy and Arms Control* (New York: Twentieth Century Fund, 1961).

[61]John Maddox and Leonard Beaton, *The Spread of Nuclear Weapons* (New York: Praeger, 1962).

direction of Grenville Clark and Louis Sohn and published in 1958 as *World Peace through World Law.*[62]

By the late 1960s an important shift began in the pattern of our programs aimed at improving conditions for world peace. We continued support for the IISS and funded a new project at the Brookings Institution to analyze the United States defense program. However, programs in international law, international training and research, world affairs education, and international organization studies were substantially reduced. The shift can be explained by a variety of factors:

1. Declining overall Foundation budgets
2. Recognition that many of the older programs had been given a vigorous start and could proceed effectively without further help from us
3. Growing doubts about the effectiveness of international law and international institutions in keeping the peace, especially in the wake of Vietnam and in light of the mounting turmoil in the developing world
4. A sense that broad citizen education for international affairs, either in colleges and universities or through public affairs groups, was a slow and uncertain way to improve understanding and to relieve world tensions
5. A mounting conviction that the most promising opportunities for improving the prospects for peace lay either in arms control achieved through international negotiation (as in the SALT talks) or direct unilateral disarmament

By the early 1970s, moreover, it became apparent to many that the achievements under SALT had been based on ideas and skills (such as those of Henry Kissinger) developed a decade before. The arms control community had been living off conceptual work carried out in 1952–1962. It was said that strategic weapons systems

---

[62]Grenville Clark and Louis Sohn, eds., *World Peace through World Law* (Cambridge, Mass.: Harvard University Press, 1958).

had "matured" but that the ideas necessary to integrate the effects of new weapons systems into the decision processes of government had not. New progress, therefore, might require an additional investment in intellectual resources. Furthermore, by 1971–72 evidence was accumulating that in the United States and other parts of the world, at many levels and in many disciplines, there was growing interest in questions related to arms control and international security. This concern, too, may be traced to the fighting in Indochina, but there was little follow-up support from either public or private funding sources.

A catalyst for a major increase in our attention to international security affairs was a period spent by the president of the Foundation at the Aspen Institute in the summer of 1972. From his discussions with a study group of the American Academy of Arts and Sciences came the idea of a major national center for international security affairs where the best minds from the United States and abroad could work on the problems of international security, train a new generation of specialists, and generate a national dialogue. We helped Harvard University establish the center. Also, in response to proposals from specialists concerned with particular aspects of international security affairs, we made smaller grants to help establish centers at MIT, Cornell, and Stanford.

In 1973 a committee of leading scholars, led by Carl Kaysen, examined the question of whether the Foundation should do even more in the field of arms control. They concluded that our program should be expanded dramatically, to about $3 million a year. A more limited program was recommended by the staff and approved by the trustees to provide several grants for a few more institutions, to sponsor a worldwide competition for innovative research proposals to train defense analysts, to support regional seminars, and to extend the program to the developing countries. This last seemed especially desirable in light of the increasing proliferation of nuclear and sophisticated conventional weapons in the developing as well as the industrialized world.

In summary, then, our program in international security and

arms control can be viewed as one response, lasting over the whole life of the Foundation, to an original objective to help improve conditions for world peace.

CASE 5.   INSTRUCTIONAL TELEVISION: MASSIVE OVERSELL

The 1950s had seemed ripe for the introduction of television as a medium of classroom instruction. School enrollment was booming, especially at the junior and senior high school levels; debate raged over the quality of education and children's grasp of basic skills; and the Soviet Union's launching of Sputnik in 1956 unleashed a frenzied effort to improve teaching, particularly in science and mathematics. Meanwhile, television had started its invasion of the American home.

Most of the staff of the Fund for the Advancement of Education, to which the Foundation had assigned the mission of school improvement, was impatient with the rank and file of the education establishment. They believed that too often schools were captives of "educationalists" who overemphasized technique and neglected content and that the cream of college graduates avoided school teaching as a career while mediocre ones drifted into it.

The Fund's staff saw television as a way of amplifying the impact of good teachers, by which they usually meant those with a strong academic background in a particular discipline. As expressed by Paul Woodring, a Fund staff member and later its historian, the objective was "to use television to bring the best teachers, the best teaching to larger numbers of students."

The Fund staff knew that they were struggling upstream. Educators had not embraced earlier technology, such as films or radio, and there was no reason to believe that they would accept television. In fact some saw it as a threat to their rule over the classroom. Moreover, television hardware was expensive, cumbersome, and still poor in technical quality.

The Fund embarked on what amounted to a massive selling job. Over a decade the Fund and the Foundation invested $30.1 million in public schools (and, to a lesser extent, in higher education) to develop instructional television wherever it had taken a precarious hold. Although the campaign was mapped by former university teachers and deans, they were careful to employ as standard bearers former schoolteachers and superintendents. Professional organizations such as the National Association of Secondary School Principals joined in, making televised instruction a major priority of its Commission on the Experimental Study of the Utilization of Staff in the Secondary School. The Commission's report, *Focus on Change,* was sent to four hundred thousand educators around the country.

The following were the principal strategies in creating, then filling, a market for instructional television.

The Fund found that the Hagerstown school system, in Washington County, Maryland, was willing to embrace televised teaching as an integral part of its instruction. Hagerstown went on to connect all its schools through closed-circuit television, and for nine years the Fund and the Foundation supported the experiment with grants totaling $1 million. Hagerstown was not only a demonstration project, although thousands of visitors, many of them sent there with Foundation assistance, made the pilgrimage to "see the future today." It was also a means of shaking down many hardware problems. Although the experiment included some conventional courses, it also provided, county-wide, specialized courses that the school system could not have afforded otherwise. County school officials viewed the televised system as a means of increasing instructional quality without increasing costs. Although the Hagerstown showcase received enormous national publicity, the model was little replicated. In the following decade and more, only a few hundred closed-circuit school systems were set up, and nearly all were far less elaborate than the one in Hagerstown.

Concurrent with the Hagerstown experiment, the Fund and the Foundation established and supported the National Program on the Use of Television in the Public Schools, which consisted of inducement grants and staff assistance to help school systems, especially in larger cities (e.g., Boston, Chicago, Denver, and San Francisco), to adopt instructional television. At first, television was to be used to teach very large classes, thus saving teacher time and classroom space while maintaining or improving the quality of instruction. Later, the National Program shifted away from its cost-saving claims, seeking instead to supplement and enrich instruction in standard-sized classes. To the limited extent that television is used in the schools now, it follows that revised pattern, remaining largely a supplementary tool of education.

The most ambitious attempt to establish a high-quality instructional television service for large numbers of students was the Midwest Program of Airborne Television Instruction (MPATI), for which $14.7 million was granted over a seven-year period. The project relied on an airplane circling over Lafayette, Indiana, that beamed television signals to some 5 million school children in six states. Many programs were especially created for that audience, but relevant outside programs were also used. The technical problems proved to be far greater than anyone had anticipated, however, and little attention was paid to how teachers might use the material. The programs were more sophisticated than those of the National Program or the Hagerstown experiment, but the participating school systems simply lacked a strong commitment to TV in the classroom. MPATI disbanded in 1967 when Foundation funds ran out. At worst it was an Edsel, at best a forerunner of instruction by satellite television, which is now being tried both in the United States and in India.

Among the open-circuit television experiments supported by the Foundation was the highly publicized program "Continental Classroom," broadcast over commercial channels ($1.7 million, 1958–1961). This program presented courses at a fairly high academic level (mathematics, physics, Shakespeare, history). The principal target audience was teachers, and at its peak "Continental Classroom" attracted some one million viewers. Over 5,000 students at one time were enrolled for credit in these courses in over 250 institutions. Today variations of "Continental Classroom" exist in some places (e.g., "Sunrise Semester" in New York City), and the use of televised programs for college credit is commonplace.

In our effort to proselytize for instructional television, we paid too little attention to course content. Indeed, when the Foundation tried in the mid-1960s to promote the use of satellite communications for public television, we still lacked a clear notion of how quality television programming would be produced.[63] Another reason for the effort's failure was that mediocre instruction over a television tube is more widely and dramatically apparent than in the traditional classroom, where it is often tolerated or goes unnoticed. Still another reason—little noted at the time—was that the typical televised instructional fare was irrelevant to the learning problems of the disadvantaged. "Sesame Street" has proved itself to be an exception, and it was developed deliberately as an out-of-school program. Its producer, the Children's Television Workshop, invested adequate funds to link educators and child-learning specialists with professional television producers, to test its programs exhaustively before they went on the air, and to conduct extensive public information and community relations programs beforehand.

That the instructional television phoenix is not permanently grounded is evident in its continuing, albeit limited, presence in some school systems and colleges and in new open learning and nontraditional programs (e.g., the Foundation-supported University of Mid-America). Further, instructional broadcasting is the major morning and early afternoon program fare of most public television stations and state networks.

[63]At least indirectly, however, Foundation activities in instructional television helped to crystallize a consensus that only a few places can produce quality ITV programs. One such place, the Agency for Instructional Television (AIT) in Bloomington, Indiana, is currently assisted by the Foundation. AIT is a consortium of state public television agencies and state departments of education. It can provide sufficient resources and a large enough market to produce quality programs.

CASE 6. GRAY AREAS/COMMUNITY DEVELOPMENT CORPORATIONS: PHILANTHROPY AS SOCIAL REFORM

The problems of the disadvantaged, primarily in the poverty enclaves of big cities but increasingly in their rural counterparts as well, have been a major Foundation concern since 1960. The Foundation programs to which they gave rise—Great Cities, Gray Areas, Community Development—each became for a time the centerpiece of the Foundation's domestic agenda. Impressive sums of money have been spent, over $25 million for Great Cities and Gray Areas and over $50 million thus far on Community Development. Equally important, this sequence of programs has been largely responsible for the public's perception of the Ford Foundation as an "up front" social welfare institution, characterized by

- An action-oriented rather than a research-oriented style, with emphasis on local demonstration projects
- A willingness to test the outer edges of advocacy and citizen participation
- A conviction that effective philanthropy requires a direct and continuing interaction between staff and grantee

In other words, the Foundation's programs for the disadvantaged have not only helped reshape public policies regarding the city and the poor, but have also been an important force in reshaping the Foundation.

Among the things that the staff has learned in supporting these programs are that all parties must be willing and able to make midcourse corrections and that it is essential to be patient about results.

Program Origins

The "disadvantaged" programs had their roots in the late 1950s. One root was in the educational crisis, the realization by the school superintendents of large cities that America's proud pub-

lic-education sector was breaking down. The other root was trace-
able to the Foundation's concern with urban and regional
development. The unprecedented wave of black and Hispanic
migrants and the out-migration of the urban middle class were
adversely affecting the capacity of the American city to carry out its
time-honored role as the staging area for socioeconomic advance.
School dropout rates and chronic welfare dependency rates were
rising; reading scores and the tax base were declining. These were
just a few skeins of a tangled web of urban pathology. Just when
the Foundation's education specialists became aware that schools
could no longer depend upon traditional pedagogy, traditional
teacher training, and traditional administrative structures, the
Foundation's urban specialists, notably Paul Ylvisaker, became
aware that traditional urban concerns—greater efficiency, more ra-
tional metropolitan structure, more competent public administration—were no longer the paths to progress. Nor did the answer lie
in an urban redevelopment philosophy that saw salvation in the
destruction and reconstruction of buildings, roads, and other
physical facilities.

These external circumstances brought on a profound reaction
in the Foundation's way of doing business. The Foundation became
activist and interventionist. Through the Great Cities educational
grants we launched a wide-ranging series of innovative projects to
make the big-city schools more responsive to their new clients,
black children of rural heritage. We discovered that school improvements would be hopelessly inadequate unless students'
problems outside the classroom were also attended to. In the Gray
Areas program we advanced the proposition that American cities
would have to invest in their residents as well as their real estate.
Comprehensiveness became the byword. Schools, jobs, housing,
health, welfare, and all other social services had to be simultaneously reformed.

Gray Areas

The main characteristics of the Gray Areas programs were—in
addition to comprehensiveness—selectivity and partnership with

government.[64] We called our approach "the social application of the art of *jujitsu*," the process of bringing small amounts of resources to bear at points of leverage to capture larger resources that would otherwise work against socially desirable ends. Selectivity was necessary because of the inherently high cost of each demonstration project ($2 million to $7 million per city) that had to come out of a limited (and reluctantly appropriated) budget. Only a few cities could be selected, and within each only a few schools or neighborhoods—and sometimes only one—could be chosen for trials. The Gray Areas programs also stressed partnership with all levels of government and established agencies. The demonstration sites chosen were those in which the political and business leaders were prepared to commit themselves to cooperation in every respect. On the winning list were Boston, New Haven, Oakland, Philadelphia, Washington, D.C., and the state of North Carolina.

The most significant outcome of the Gray Areas programs was that, together with projects funded by the President's Committee on Juvenile Delinquency and with advances in civil rights, it became the working model of the federal government's Great Society programs. Great Society efforts in education, manpower, legal services, housing, health services, and community action were clearly borrowed from these earlier pilot programs. Though opinion remains divided about the ultimate outcome of the Great Society, Gray Areas is an unusually clear example of how a private foundation can serve as the leading edge of social reform.

The Gray Areas experience also had its sobering side, however. To summarize very briefly three of the lessons for Foundation managers:

---

[64]Before it fades from memory, we would like to record the origin of the label. Ylvisaker borrowed it from Raymond Vernon, who in the mid-1950s had conducted a series of Foundation-supported studies of the New York region. Vernon invented the term to distinguish those areas falling between the city's prime areas, which did not need intervention, and its hopeless slums, which were too far gone for intervention. The appropriate places for intervention, he believed, were the in-between areas of incipient decline. The South Bronx was one of his candidates, which just goes to show how long ago all this was and how hard is the lot of the urban prognosticator.

1. As is true with almost everything else we do, quality of leadership was paramount. But, in this untried enterprise it was not easy to define, in advance, the right mix of abilities, and mistakes were made. Most was achieved in those localities where both the chief elected official and the head of the Gray Areas corporations were honest in commitment and competent in management. New Haven did much better than Philadelphia.

2. Experience showed that these extraordinarily wide-ranging programs could not be usefully evaluated by such terms as "success" or "failure." It was necessary to produce a separate scorecard for each major component. One place might do better on schools or housing and less well in manpower or grassroots participation; another might show opposite results.

3. The close involvement of Foundation staff had drawbacks as well as gains. Overzealous or overdetailed regulation and the habit of changing signals often impaired the effectivness and sometimes the credibility of the grantee organization with respect to its target constituents.

With the advent of the Great Society and Office of Economic Opportunity programs in the mid-1960s, Gray Areas was gradually phased out, to be supplanted by experiments with Community Development Corporations (CDCs).

Community Development Corporations

The essential differences between the Gray Areas programs and the Community Development Corporations program are not in fundamental objectives; like Gray Areas, the CDC program aims at improving the circumstances of the disadvantaged; the differences lie, rather, in the relationship with government. Gray Areas was essentially an *adjunct* to government that concentrated on social service programs; CDC is a *proxy* for local government, concentrating much more on economic development and on residential and commercial building and renewal, a distinction of considerable significance.

The rapid national proliferation of poverty programs in the

1960s overwhelmed the administrative capacities of state and local government. Similar failures emerged in Model Cities and Community Action, the federal government's two efforts to substitute a grassroots management scheme for conventional local government agencies. Model Cities and Community Action fell victim to the same ills from which public administration suffered, promises that exceeded performance, managers appointed for patronage rather than competence, press releases produced instead of housing. Something better was needed, a management device that could combine the professional skills one might expect from government (minus the restrictions of civil service and inflexible regulations) with the decentralized autonomy, street wisdom, motivation, and local pride that might be found in a community organization.

The essential difference between the CDC program and other proxy organizations like Community Action and Model Cities is the heavy emphasis of CDC on product rather than on process: A couple of hundred housing units is worth more than "telling whitey off."

Results of the CDC effort thus far indicate that, as in Gray Areas, the quality of leadership is the crucial ingredient. Again, too, evaluation has to be done component by component. Thus, minority enterprise did not fare well in Philadelphia, but is doing fine in the Mississippi Delta; retail stores have done well in the Bedford-Stuyvesant area of Brooklyn but not in Watts; housing is doing well in both Watts and Bed-Stuy, but not, as yet, in Alabama. Transcending these details is the more fundamental result. To a measurable degree, although not without cyclical setbacks, disadvantaged minorities are moving up the social, educational, and economic ladders. Still, an uncounted but substantial minority of a minority is left behind, a hard core of people and families with pronounced traits of incompetence, dependency, and crime who are seemingly immune to known remedies. This fact is, once again, causing a shift in the Foundation's priorities; we have embarked on a new series of programs targeted on these residual groups, programs such as Supported Work and Tenant Management.

CASE 7.   FEDERAL EXECUTIVE TRAINING: THE HIGHER GENERALISM

Beginning in 1955 the Foundation supported several experiments in midcareer training and education for high-level federal employees. These programs are now an established part of the training activities of the U.S. Civil Service Commission. Our grants totaled $2.6 million, approximately half of which went to the National Institute of Public Affairs (NIPA).[65]

The Foundation did not originate the idea of midcareer training for government executives; the notion was already in the wind when we took our first steps. But it is fair to say that our support strengthened the movement and hastened its adoption as government policy.

In the mid-1950s there was growing recognition that the explosive growth of information relevant to managerial decisions required periodic "retooling" of the people who run large organizations in both the private and the public sectors. In the public sector the first halting steps were taken with the report of the second Hoover Commission in 1955.[66] It called for the creation of a "higher civil service" comprising the most capable executives in the federal government. To bring this about, the commission proposed a program of midcareer education, financed by the federal government, that would make available to federal managers opportunities for sharpening their skills and acquiring advanced education in management and administration. In 1958 Congress passed the Federal Employees' Training Act, providing financial support for executive training for the first time.

A year before the Hoover Commission report, in 1954, the Foundation supported an American Assembly on "The Federal Government Service: Its Character, Prestige, and Problems." This

[65]Other recipients were the American Political Science Association, the Brookings Institution, the University of Virginia, Columbia University, and the University of Chicago.

[66]The commission's staff included George Graham and William Pincus, who later became the architects of the Foundation's federal training program.

was followed by our first substantial action in the field, a grant to the Brookings Institution to provide "policy leadership training" to selected high-level federal civil servants through one- to two-week conferences held in Williamsburg, Virginia. At the meetings, small groups of bureaucrats intensively explored basic social, economic, and political trends and their implications for the management of federal agencies and programs. This project marked Brookings's entry into a field that has since become one of its mainstays.

A somewhat different approach is illustrated by a Foundation-assisted program of summer institutes run by the University of Chicago to provide executive development for federal administrators. Modeled after university programs for corporate executives, these seminars brought to their participants the latest advances in management science.

A basic issue in executive development is the choice between specialized technical training and broader, more generalized educational programs. The competition between these approaches is particularly acute in the public sector. The great majority of top public administrators began their careers as technical specialists— biological and physical scientists, engineers, lawyers, physicians, economists, and the like. Few have been trained as managers. The Federal Employees' Training Act was conceived as a vehicle for increasing federal employees' specialized technical skills, emphasizing refresher courses in the traditional professional disciplines. The Foundation program, in contrast, was designed to assure that adequate attention was given the other side of the equation, education of a much broader, more general sort. Our grants sought to turn specialitsts who had risen to high administrative positions into the type of generalist executive that these new positions required.

The most ambitious of the Foundation-supported programs was initiated in 1962 with a $1.25 million grant to the National Institute of Public Affairs for its Career Education Awards. Linked directly to the Federal Employees' Training Act, this program annually placed approximately eighty top federal executives at selected universities where they spent a full academic year taking courses that would fill gaps in their educational background, broaden their perspectives, and enhance their administrative skills.[67] The Foundation grant permitted NIPA to assist in the selection of candidates, negotiate with participating universities, advise employees on which institution to choose, arrange orientation sessions, and subsidize some of the extraordinary costs associated with a year away from the job. The employing federal agency used Training Act funds to pay participants their full salaries during the academic year. In the five years of the program, over four hundred public employees participated; more than 90 percent were top federal executives, with the others being drawn from state and local government.

A parallel program for permanent staff members of the Congress was tried with a grant of $628,000 to the American Political Science Association in 1963; it was handicapped from the beginning because Congress would not pay the salaries of staff members who took part. The program collapsed when Foundation support ended.

In addition to this series of grants, the Foundation supported a research effort by the Brookings Institution that examined the nature and needs of the federal service from several new perspectives. The Brookings's project resulted in the publication during the early 1960s of three pathbreaking studies: David Stanley's *The Higher Civil Service: An Evaluation of Federal Personnel Problems*,[68] Mann and Doig's *The Assistant Secretaries: Problems and Processes of Appointment*,[69] and a report on a national citizen survey, *The Image of the Federal Service*.[70]

The impact of the whole executive training effort is still clearly

[67]The universities involved were Chicago, Cornell, Harvard, Indiana, Princeton, Stanford, Southern California, Virginia, and Washington.

[68]David Stanley, *The Higher Civil Service: An Evaluation of Federal Personnel Problems* (Washington, D.C.: Brookings Institution, 1964).

[69]Dean E. Mann and Jameson W. Doig, *The Assistant Secretaries: Problems and Processes of Appointment* (Washington, D.C.: Brookings Institution, 1965).

[70]Franklin P. Kilpatrick, *The Image of the Federal Service* (Washington, D.C.: Brookings Institution, 1964).

visible fifteen years after the last grant was made in 1963. Brookings's earlier seminars for federal executives led to the creation of its Advanced Study program for federal and business executives, which is entirely supported by federal agencies and the larger corporations. Brookings now also conducts training programs for members and professional staff of the Congress under a contract with the Congressional Research Service. The NIPA Career Education Awards program has been taken over by the Civil Service Commission and is now firmly institutionalized and wholly funded from federal appropriations. Although the University of Chicago no longer conducts its summer institutes for federal executives, the project director of that effort is now at New York University, where he has developed a series of management institutes for state and local public managers modeled after the Chicago program. Also indicative of the federal commitment to training was the establishment six years ago of the Federal Executive Institute (FEI), a residential training program. In addition to the contribution that Foundation-supported programs made to the planning of FEI, a grant to the University of Virginia in 1969 provided some $100,000 for the participation of university faculty during FEI's early years.

CASE 8. RESIDENT THEATERS / BALLET COMPANIES: FINANCIAL DISCIPLINE

The Foundation's program of major operating support for performing arts companies began in 1962, five years after the Humanities and Arts Division was formed. We concentrated on helping theater and ballet companies mainly because they seemed to need the most help at the time, and because we thought that investment in these fields presented the greatest opportunity to make an important contribution to the cultural life of the country. Since 1962 grants totaling $17.7 million have gone to fifteen resident theaters and $14.7 million to seven ballet companies. These amounts were for operating or capital support or both.[71]

Looking back now, with vision considerably sharpened by hindsight and experience, it is fair to say that we might have helped the same number of companies with less money *or* helped more companies with the same amount if we had insisted on two things:

1. Rigorously formulated, long-range financial plans drawn up by the companies and scrutinized by us to determine their completeness and feasibility. Perhaps most if not all of the failures in the program could have been avoided thereby, and the successes might have been achieved with smaller Foundation investment.
2. Provisions similar to those in our cash reserve grants, which enforce financial discipline on the grantee companies. There was too great a tendency on the part of the grantees to regard the Foundation as a cushion that they could always fall back on. If, instead, they had been required from the beginning to do more to prepare for the day when we would not be there, that day probably would have arrived sooner and the companies would have been in a stronger position when the time came to cut the cord.

When the Foundation began helping performing arts companies—the symphony and the opera as well as the theater and ballet—the situations of the four fields were quite different. Symphony orchestras had their problems, but they were the most firmly established performing companies in the country, with a history of some seventy-five years of growth and development.

[71]Totals do not include cash reserve grants, which are not for operating support, nor do they include grants to theater workshops such as La Mama and the Chelsea Theater Center, to companies with special social development objectives such as the Negro Ensemble Company and the Dance Theatre of Harlem, or to the resident theaters for such special purposes as supporting playwrights in residence. Were these to be included, the total Foundation support in theater and dance would be $70.8 million.

p management of the Foundation in 1952. Left to right, Henry Ford II, chairman of the Board of Trustees;
ul G. Hoffman, president and director; and associate directors Chester C. Davis, Robert M. Hutchins,
d H. Rowan Gaither, Jr. (Fourth associate director, Milton Katz, not shown).

enty years later. McGeorge Bundy (left), president of the Foundation, and Alexander Heard, chairman
the Board of Trustees.

From the 1950s: Left, Harvard's was one of several graduate schools of business aided in efforts to modernize management education. Center, the Foundation joined the National Science Foundation in financing a 158-inch optical telescope in Chile. Below, mental health research programs included grants for Bruno Bettleheim's work at the Sonia Shankman Orthogenic School in Chicago.

igh school students in Illinois in 1958 take examination for National Merit Scholarships. Another Founda-
on-supported educational effort . . .

, sought to improve methods of teaching disadvantaged children, such as those shown here in
-sburgh's Miller School.

Improved opportunities for minorities in higher education was a major objective in the 1970s. Half of a six-year, $100 million program assisted a selected group of private black colleges. Recipients included the Atlanta University Center (library shown here), which consists of six institutions.

eam teaching was stimulated by the Foundation offshoot, the Fund for the Advancement of Education. In his Pittsburgh school a team of thirteen teachers, including subject specialists, served the classes shown in he background.

llowships and internships afforded graduate students and other young people practical experience in vernment. Here college graduates discuss careers in public affairs with a San Francisco labor official.

Assistance to minority self-help organizations has been a major Foundation activity. This meeting was associated with the North Carolina Fund, an early anti-poverty program. Another recipient was the Bedford-Stuyvesant Restoration Corporation, Brooklyn, New York (opposite).

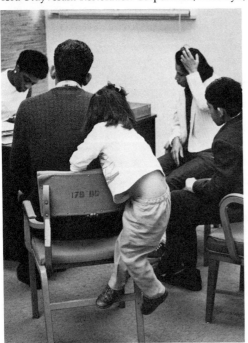

Chicano family seeks help from Denver fair-housing organization (left). Women's Law Fund lawyer counsels client (right). The fund is one of many activities assisted to advance the status of women.

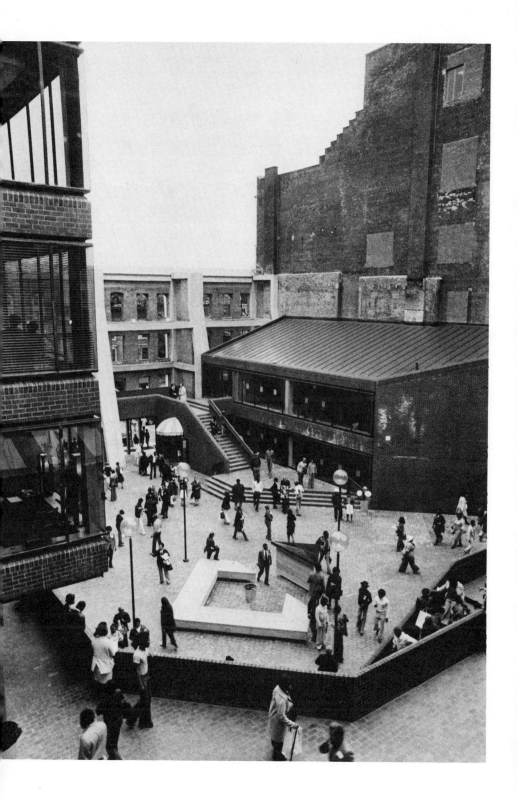

The adaptation of television to educational and cultural uses has been a major focus for Foundation support. In the 1950s the noted series *Omnibus* (above, featuring Alistair Cooke) . . . and later the Children's Television Workshop's popular "Sesame Street," starring Big Bird.

he development of strong ballet companies in the United States was supported heavily in the 1950s and 960s. Here George Balanchine, celebrated choreographer, and Jacques d'Amboise, dancer and choreog-apher, rehearse dancers from the New York City Ballet.

In one of its largest actions, the Foundation committed $80.2 million for sixty-one symphony orchestras including the Los Angeles Philharmonic, conducted by Zubin Mehta.

The Alley Theater, Houston, one of several resident, professional, noncommercial theaters whose development was assisted for some twenty years.

uwannee River in Florida, one of many natural reas protected by the Nature Conservancy, vhich was supported in the 1960s. Below, parcipants in the National Coal Policy Project view eclamation site in a strip-mined area. The Founation has sought to improve communication mong parties in energy issues and disputes.

International activities have included support of human rights (such as funds for refugees from East Germany, top, in the early 1950s) and assistance to educational institutions in the less developed countries, such as the American University of Beirut, middle.

Advanced students at Cornell University receiv Chinese-language instruction. Through the 195(and 1960s, the Foundation granted some $25 million to advance American knowledge of nor Western societies and international affairs.

University of Ghana instructor teaching administrative principles. The Foundation helped newly independent African countries upgrade their civil service personnel.

A wide variety of research was supported to improve agricultural productivity and rural life and thereby stem migration to urban areas, such as this shantytown outside Rio de Janeiro.

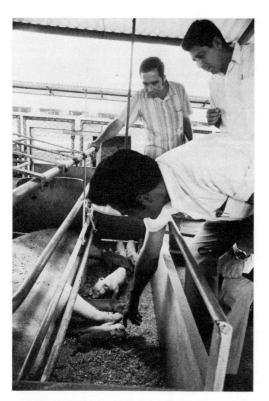

The Foundation has assisted nine internationa agricultural research centers in an effort to appl science and technology to the challenge of in creasing world food supplies. Among them ar the International Center for Tropical Agricultur in Palmira, Colombia (left) and the Internation Institute of Tropical Agriculture in Ibadan, oppc site. Below, wheat harvest in the Punjab, 196 Wheat production in India rose dramatically in th late 1960s and early 1970s — from 11 million 22.8 million metric tons annually — but Asia countries are hard pressed to increase food pr duction to keep pace with burgeoning popul; tions.

In the 1960s, the Foundation became the leading private source of support for biomedical research aimed at improved methods of birth control. Among the recipients was Dr. Egon Diczfalusy, a noted Swedish endocrinologist, shown here giving a seminar for scientists from several countries.

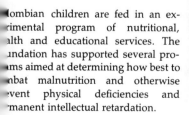

ombian children are fed in an ex-
rimental program of nutritional,
alth and educational services. The
ndation has supported several pro-
ms aimed at determining how best to
nbat malnutrition and otherwise
vent physical deficiencies and
manent intellectual retardation.

"My project, boiled down to its essentials, is simply this, sir. I want to determine, once and for all, whether there is any truth in the common belief that money can't buy happiness."

Drawing by D. Fradon; © 1963, The New Yorker Magazine, Inc.

Drawing by Lorenz; © 1964, The New Yorker Magazine, Inc.

Opera companies were by no means as established as orchestras, but there were a number of reputable companies, major ones in New York, Chicago, and San Francisco, and fifteen to twenty so-called civic operas with very short but regular seasons and sufficient community support to ensure them important niches in their cities' cultural life.[72]

The case of theaters and ballet companies was much more precarious. Serious new drama had virtually disappeared from Broadway, which had turned more and more to musicals and light entertainment, largely because the high costs of production made investors shy away from risky ventures and hanker after sure-fire hits. Outside New York, however, a new phenomenon, the resident theater, was beginning to show real promise. Although some resident theaters were running on a shoestring and performing in spartan surroundings, they were achieving a high degree of artistry. They made it seem possible that theater in America could be a cultural as well as a commercial resource, one that ranked in importance with music, literature, or the visual arts. At the time, it should be recalled, the National Endowment for the Arts had not institutions that would set national artistic standards and, by exam-councils in existence. Few private foundations allocated funds to the performing arts, and even those that did, such as the Rockefeller Foundation from 1963 onward, had budgets too small to commit operating funds to major institution-building programs. The Ford Foundation was thus one of the few sources for the kind of risk capital that fledgling companies needed to enhance their artistry and fully establish themselves as professional theaters.

As for ballet, there were only three professional companies in the country: the New York City Ballet, the San Francisco Ballet,

[72]From 1963 through 1966 the Foundation provided $4.2 million to operas, principally to lengthen the seasons of civic operas, and in 1974 $2.1 million was granted for general support of the New York City Opera. The very large ($80 million) symphony orchestra program of 1965 was mentioned in the first part of this report; it was possible only because of the availability of extra funds apart from regular program budgets and therefore was unique in the history of our arts program.

and the American Ballet Theatre. There were also some fifty "civic" ballets, giving one or two performances a year and drawing upon the talents of teachers and students from local schools where the training was often poor. Although ballet was beginning to attract interest throughout the country, the field was woefully underdeveloped.

The selection process was relatively simple, though protracted. Staff members traveled round the country, familiarizing themselves with the problems and potentials of the various groups, and they also sought the advice of people knowledgeable in the fields. Negotiations with the companies were long and detailed, particularly over questions of the exact amount of matching requirements, which were a feature of most of the grants. No advisory committees were set up because there were too few possible candidates to require that kind of formal screening.

The theater and ballet grants were intended to help develop institutions that would set national artistic standards and, by example, stimulate similar developments in other localities. Generally the program was successful. Among the notable successes was the Pennsylvania Ballet; led by an exceptionally capable director, it developed from scratch into a company of the highest quality. Among the failures, the most notable was the Mummers Theatre in Oklahoma City, a community theater that was planning to become professional when housed in an urban renewal development. But the project was delayed interminably, costs escalated, and in the end the theater's board was unwilling or unable to raise sufficient funds to keep the Mummers alive.

All in all, the grants accomplished more than their immediate objective. A group of standard-setters is in place. The resident theaters have demonstrated that they can draw audiences and win community support as they come to be regarded as cultural assets. Encouraged by this demonstration, other resident theaters have been founded, and there are now some forty in existence as compared with about a half dozen in the early 1960s. In ballet there are now eight professional companies, most of them Foundation grantees, and a number of civic companies are approaching professional rank.

The original idea of these grants was to help institutions grow or improve; therefore, budget increases were required, and we made operating support grants. But such grants create dependency, which means making successive grants to the same organizations, thus limiting the number of companies we can help. In the 1960s there were only a few companies with the artistic potential to benefit from the Foundation's program. Today, with far more in the field than the Foundation could hope to assist, the need is for better management and financial stability. For these reasons we began in the 1970s to negotiate terminal grants with our dependents, while at the same time seeking ways to help stabilize them. In the process we evolved the cash reserve program, which we are learning to use as the core of an effort to promote institutional stability by improving fiscal management. Operas and modern dance companies are also included in this effort.

The cash reserve grant is of practical utility in a number of ways, beginning with the elimination of cash flow crises. More important, it provides a powerful incentive for companies to manage their affairs so that they end each fiscal year in the black, a status that had eluded many of them. We require them to adopt rigorous budget controls and help them to do so. For example, we have a consulting accountant who not only helps us monitor the grants but also helps the companies with their budgetary and other financial problems. Their budgets must reflect a long-range plan that translates artistic objectives and the means of attaining them into dollar terms, makes complete and realistic estimates of the income obtainable from different sources to meet these needs, and adjusts accordingly.

Our experience to date has convinced us that sound long-range planning is essential to orderly growth and financial stability in the performing arts. Our present strategy of institutional support, almost all of it through cash reserve grants, encourages such planning.

CASE 9.   AMERICAN STUDIES IN EUROPE: A CHANGING CULTURAL CLIMATE

Since the mid-1950s, the Foundation has granted approximately $9 million to help advance understanding of American culture and institutions in Europe.

This program is notable for, among other things, the manner in which its goals (stated and implicit) have shifted over the years in response to changes in the domestic and European cultural and ideological climates. Another characteristic of the program has been its use of a single subcontractor, the American Council of Learned Societies (ACLS), for the bulk of the work.

When the first major grants for American studies were made, there was a prevailing sense that the United States held a preeminent position (1) in the Western alliance in the Cold War, (2) in the development of new technology and effective social and political institutions, and (3) in most of the academic disciplines. This attitude was strong enough in Europe that there was a generally positive response to the Foundation's initiative. The early grants had both an international relations objective—to strengthen the free world through mutual understanding—and a developmental objective—to assist the Europeans in adapting American models to their institutions.

By the late 1960s we had begun to reexamine the initial objectives of the American Studies programs. American self-confidence was declining, and so was European confidence in the American capacity to lead either politically or culturally. Some Foundation staff, embarrassed by certain American foreign policies, actually came to oppose support of American Studies programs abroad. Two new objectives for our support of these programs were adopted: (1) a joint search by Europeans and Americans for common approaches to common problems; and (2) temporary sustenance of scholars and of the more successful institutions that had been created during the 1960s while they sought alternative sources of support. One implication of these changes was a shift in the focus of the programs from history and literature (with their orientation toward American experience and achievements) to the policy-oriented social sciences.

With grants from us totaling $9.3 million, from 1961 through 1975, the ACLS used a wide range of instruments to develop the American Studies programs abroad, particularly in Europe. Guided by advisory committees of scholars from Europe and the United States, it provided partial endowment for university chairs, funds for library acquisitions at European universities, fellowships for Europeans to study in the United States, and general encouragement to American studies associations and other networks.

Our subcontracting to the ACLS provided unusual program continuity. The same program manager was in charge over the full fifteen years. In addition, the Foundation was able to maintain a low profile in the making of grants to individuals and institutions, which would not have been possible under in-house management. At the same time, the ACLS has been adaptable, responding to changing social perceptions and Foundation priorities. For example, institutional development (professorships and libraries) has gradually been supplanted by fellowships to individuals.

Other actions reflecting the American Studies program goals have included:

1. *Direct grants for support of university centers,* notably those totaling $650,000 to the Free University of Berlin for the John F. Kennedy Institute of American Studies, and another providing $228,000 to the University of London to strengthen teaching resources in American law.

2. *Seminars,* and above all the Salzburg Seminar in American Studies to which we have given $1,045,000 since 1955. Aimed at "young professional leaders," the program consists of informal short courses for young Europeans. Here, too, when the concept of American Studies shifted in the late 1960s, the seminar's syllabus reflected that shift from "American institutions" to "common

problems" of interest to Europeans and Americans. A summer seminar run for a number of years by Henry Kissinger at Harvard was also concerned with exposing young foreign leaders to American culture and institutions.

3. *Individualized exchange programs,* such as the Eisenhower Fellowships and those of the English-Speaking Union, the Institute of Contemporary Arts, the Institute of International Education, the American Scandinavian Foundation, and the Governmental Affairs Institute.

4. *Miscellaneous grants* that, in addition to their more obvious goals, appear to have had some American studies purpose, e.g., $250,000 to Athens College to strengthen its American teaching staff, $19,000 to the Boston Symphony Orchestra for visits by European composers, and grants totaling $179,000 to the Carnegie Endowment for a series of Bilderberg conferences of leaders from North America and Western Europe.

5. *Elements of programs given other designations,* e.g., improvements in higher education in Europe that have included the input of American expertise.

Although it is impossible to distinguish the results of Foundation contributions to European understanding of American affairs from those of other sponsors and from unsponsored spontaneous activity, the Foundation did loom large in the total picture. In general it appears that communities of sophisticated specialists in United States affairs have been successfully created and nurtured in most countries of Western Europe (and to a lesser extent even in the East). Many of the large and conspicuous American studies centers, notably the Kennedy Institute in Berlin, did not prosper and were victims of the anti-Americanism and university turmoil of the late 1960s and early 1970s. But the individual specialists have continued to multiply and to ply their trade. Moreover, the movement seems now to be self-sustaining. In the last few years, for the first time since Brogan, European experts on American history, society, and institutions have begun to command the serious respect that the United States once accorded Tocqueville and Bryce.

Most of these new scholars have been touched by our programs at some point in their careers.

The indirect effects of these programs are even harder to assess than the direct ones. It is possible only to guess whether international relations have been improved or common problems solved through the Foundation's efforts. Some of us who were not here when it all began believe that the impact was real, important, and will endure well past our own time.

Our withdrawal from American studies in Europe in the 1970s can be explained in terms of at least three developments: (1) a changed perception of the importance of the Atlantic Alliance; (2) a decision to assist common problem-solving through more finely targeted programs; and (3) a sense that after twenty years, even with the best programs, it is time to move on. In the most important cases, the ACLS programs and the Salzburg Seminar, efforts were made to effect withdrawal in a way and at a pace that would permit other funds to be brought in to fill the gap. In both cases survival seems probable, although not assured.

The federal government has been the only other American source of substantial funds for American studies in Europe. At various times it was hoped that the government would some day take over much of the burden from the Foundation. Apart from some contributions under the Fulbright program, the hope has not materialized.

Case 10. Cooperative Education: Expanding a Concept

Cooperative education, a system in which college students alternate between periods of study and periods of planned, supervised employment related to their studies, predated the Foundation by nearly a half century. However, it had been limited to a few dozen institutions and, with such exceptions as Antioch (one of the few liberal arts colleges that embraced the concept), generally lacked repute in higher education. The Fund for the Advancement of Education and the Foundation were responsible for research that documented the caliber of existing cooperative education programs, for demonstrating the usefulness of the concept for minorities and other disadvantaged students, for expanding cooperative education to a much wider range of institutions, and for enlisting increased federal support for the idea.

The Foundation worked on cooperative education intermittently from 1958 through 1971, spending approximately $1.7 million. Our assistance took three forms:

1. Support of basic studies of the concept
2. Assistance to two waves of demonstration projects
3. Support at a critical period to the national coordinating body in the field

Our participation began in 1957 when Clarence Faust, president of the Fund for the Advancement of Education (and later, a vice-president of the Ford Foundation as well), was invited to address the first national meeting on cooperative education, convened by the Kettering Foundation and the Thomas Alva Edison Foundation. Faust, a former dean of the college at the University of Chicago, had been invited by a former Chicago faculty member and Edison Foundation official, George Probst. Faust emerged from the conference, which was attended by 300 employers and educators, sufficiently impressed with the cooperative idea to commit the Fund to a two-year study of the field. The study, headed by Ralph W. Tyler, director of the Center for Advanced Study in the Behavioral Sciences, was designed to provide a solid factual base validating further support. As one means of implementing the study's recommendations, the Kettering Foundation in 1962 helped establish the National Commission for Cooperative Education, a continuing center of information, consulting services, and promotion.

At the time forty-five institutions of higher education offered cooperative education to about 23,000 students. Today, more than 900 institutions enroll some 200,000 students in such programs. Once largely confined to engineering, science, and business education, the cooperative system has spread to nearly every academic field.

In the late 1950s we viewed the concept as a possible means of coping with the huge wave of students then approaching college age, those born during the "baby boom" of the late 1940s. Since half the students in cooperative education are away from the campus at work, it was reasoned, colleges could double their enrollments without expanding their physical facilities. This hopeful estimate did not turn out to be the principal benefit of the expanded movement.

In the mid-1960s, as philanthropic consciousness about the disadvantaged emerged, the Fund made grants (in the $50,000–$60,000 range) to implant the cooperative education idea in institutions, over a wide geographic area, that served minority students and others from lower-income families. A Foundation evaluation of these grants by consultants came to these conclusions:

1. Technical education could be provided without heavy investments in equipment.
2. The cooperative education program provided a new basis for support from industry.
3. Cooperative education could, as the Tyler report had suggested, materially help low-income students finance their college education. (At Northeastern University in Boston, for example, on-the-job earnings by disadvantaged students nearly doubled the value of scholarship aid.)
4. Cooperative education could help foundering institutions attract students. (Wilberforce University, a predominantly black institution near Dayton, Ohio, reported that cooperative education had increased its enrollment by almost 40 percent.)

When the Fund for the Advancement of Education began winding up its affairs in the 1960s, however, the Foundation turned down requests for renewed support of cooperative education. Then, with the arrival of a new Foundation administration in

1966, the education staff revived the subject. The Foundation picked up support of the National Commission as the commission's five-year backing by the Kettering Foundation was drawing to an end. Some financial aid came from a few corporations (e.g., IBM, Union Carbide, General Electric, Atlantic Richfield, and the Big Three of the auto industry). However, the Foundation's support was crucial to the ability of the commission ultimately to affect federal policy. Also, the Foundation supported another round of demonstration projects. Grants to two of the earlier recipients were supplemented, and five more institutions were added to the roster. The new group provided diversity; it included, for example, a state university (Rutgers).[73] As a means of giving greater status to the field, we helped endow a research professorship at Northeastern University, which earlier, also with our assistance, had set up a consulting service in cooperative education.

The agreement of the recipient institutions to try cooperative education represented a substantial commitment since it requires large institutional alterations.

Although the commission was not organized to lobby for federal support of cooperative education, the concept was brought to congressional attention by Ralph Tyler at the request of Wilbur Cohen, then Undersecretary of Health, Education and Welfare.

The experience drawn from the Foundation-supported programs provided the base for the commission's legislative recommendations. In 1968 and 1969, the White House, the U.S. Office of Education, and congressional committees sought information and research data on successful models and other documentary material from the commission. Cooperative education was written into the Higher Education Act of 1965 and into the amendments of 1968 and 1972. The Cooperative Education section of the act now provides $10.75 million annually for institutions wishing to develop cooperative education programs. Recipients include community

---

[73]One of the recipients, incidentally, provided us with a handy rejoinder to the charge that we traffic only with blue-chip institutions: the Neosho Water and Sewerage Technical School, Neosho, Missouri, one of the country's foremost proprietary technical schools.

colleges, liberal arts and specialized private and public colleges, and state universities.

In recent years cooperative-education students in the United States have earned more than $500 million. The less tangible yields are the heightened academic motivation students have when alternating and integrating work with on-campus study, the closer ties they perceive between theory and practice, the greater sense of responsibility they feel, and the earlier orientation they gain to the world of work. Congress has consistently appropriated the full funds authorized for cooperative education. The commission attributes this to the fact that the program returns to the government (in the form of taxes on student income from the work phase of the program) more than the government spends.

CASE 11.   HOUSING: CONCRETENESS AND ABSTRACTION

Housing was not originally envisaged as a field of interest for the Ford Foundation. A few housing research grants were made in the 1950s, including $250,000 in 1955 to the American Council to Improve Our Neighborhoods, Inc., and lesser amounts to study the housing problems of the aged. But it was not until well into the 1960s that we began a sustained program on the subject. We entered the field after Congress had enacted a huge subsidy program for low- and moderate-income housing construction. The hitch was that nonprofit housing sponsors were made eligible for the most favorable mortages, and few of them had the technical expertise to use their money to best effect. Robert Weaver, a former Foundation staff member then with the Johnson administration, appealed to us for help in providing the necessary skills to the nonprofit housing groups. Action, Inc., of Pittsburgh surveyed the field under a small Foundation grant ($25,000) and essentially ratified Weaver's belief that assistance was needed. We then launched our program.

Since then, with grants and program-related investments totaling $31.5 million, we have supported a variety of efforts aimed at two broad goals: (1) the construction of more low/moderate-income housing (in more recent years, construction has given way to programs devoted to the management and preservation of existing housing), and (2) improving minority access to decent housing.

Even limited results in either area are remarkable given the magnitude of housing problems in the United States. For one thing, housing is a multibillion-dollar profit-motivated enterprise. For another, we have had to contend against powerful demographic and attitudinal forces, including racial discrimination.

Over the years, government actions have greatly improved our ability to help. With respect to increasing the supply of housing, our relations with government have grown more intimate. In trying to widen minority access, we work only in the private (largely nonprofit) sector, but government action and judicial decisions have made the climate far more hospitable than when we began.

Housing Inventory

Our first efforts in the category of housing inventory aimed at expanded production. After achieving some success there, we turned to the related mission of preserving or rehabilitating housing.

Production. In aiming to expand production we started by trying to help supply needed skills for private housing sponsors and developers organized as limited-dividend or nonprofit corporations. We helped set up a national technical advisory service, known after several name changes as the Nonprofit Housing Center. Under grants totaling $3.4 million (1964–1973), the center conducted training workshops and conferences, provided field services, and made seed money loans enabling hundreds of development corporations and sponsors to participate in the federal subsidy programs. We also helped set up a few intermediary organizations (in three states and five cities) to provide technical assistance at the state and metropolitan levels.

We made a particular effort in rural housing, which is generally in worse condition than urban housing. The bulk of our funds in this field ($950,000 of $1.2 million) went to the Rural Housing Alliance, a national organization that provides technical assistance in rural areas comparable to what the Nonprofit Housing Center provided for urban housing. The remainder went for support of local self-help housing demonstration projects in Mississippi and California.

The Foundation also assisted local experiments in training and research in the production of low- and moderate-income housing, and it made a few grants for inner-city reconstruction that included housing development components. The Foundation's support of Community Development Corporation activities are now the only vestige of our presence in the housing production field.

As the cadre of trainee housing specialists grew in numbers and sophistication, housing development corporations and local sponsors produced subsidized homes and apartments at a rate that began to approach the national goal of 600,000 new subsidized units a year.

But there is a sad postscript. In January 1973, the federal government announced a moratorium on all further commitments under most urban aid programs administered by the Department of Housing and Urban Development (HUD), including the principal housing subsidy programs. The moratorium was triggered by disclosures of high failure rates in subsidized housing projects and of occasional instances of corruption and mismangement in the single-family-home program. It also reflected the administration's concern over the program's high cost and its desire to spur Congress to pass revenue-sharing legislation, which would transfer responsibility for urban aid to state and local governments. The construction boom in low- and moderate-income housing was stopped in its tracks and the network of private-sector supports that the Foundation had helped put in place became obsolete.

Preservation. But even before the moratorium, success had in a sense bred failure. By 1972 the many new subsidized housing units had serious problems, including rapidly rising maintenance costs, poor management of multifamily projects, and inadequate preparation of the new units' occupants for their responsibilities as tenants or homeowners.

Accordingly, our emphasis shifted from a single-minded concern with quantity to a greater concern with what happens to the housing after it is built. The Foundation has since supported home ownership counseling, management training, research on design, and tenant management programs. We have helped a St. Louis group demonstrate that tenant management can save public housing projects from deterioration and abandonment. The success of that program has led to the development of other tenant management demonstrations in six cities. They combine improved operation of public housing with job opportunities in housing complexes for hard-to-employ residents. Foundation support of $600,000 for this demonstration program has unlocked a commitment of $20.2 million from HUD.

Another approach to housing preservation, called Neighborhood Housing Services (NHS), addresses the problem of rehabilitating homes in declining neighborhoods that financial institutions have red-lined, that is, judged too risky for loan or mortgage investment. NHS involves homeowners, local lending institutions, city government, foundations, and a small, professionally staffed housing center in systematic upgrading of all substandard homes in a neighborhood. Pittsburgh pioneered the program with support from the Richard King Mellon Foundation, and it is now in operation in sixteen cities. The Foundation provided matching funds for early demonstrations in Oakland, Washington, Dallas, Baltimore, and San Antonio. Development of additional NHS programs is going forward under a major commitment of HUD funds, thus enabling the Foundation to phase out its support.

Our current emphasis on preserving older housing has been reinforced by other important trends. One is the decline of population in central cities; new housing is less needed than is improved housing. Also, the vicissitudes of the market for multifamily mortgages and for state-agency housing bonds and the very sharp

rise in apartment construction and maintenance costs have all
made refurbishing older housing more economic than building
new housing.

Foundation grants and projects for housing preservation now
total $5.4 million.

Open Housing

Despite major legislative and court victories since we made our
first grants in 1966, open housing remains for many people more
an abstract right than a marketplace reality. Most blacks seeking
homes outside the central city move to close-in transitional
neighborhoods, "escape corridors," or traditional black enclaves.
To live elsewhere, they almost always need extraordinary persistence and the aid of a local fair-housing group. The unremitting
efforts of a strong open housing movement are needed today as
much as ever.

Respected analysts tell us that to date there is no evidence of
more than modest shifts in the residential isolation of blacks. In
some metropolitan areas blacks have found themselves as segre-
gated in the suburbs as in the central city, albeit with better housing and with access to better schools and jobs. Prospects for change
in the 1970s and 1980s depend on the nation's efforts to reduce
continuing discrimination in the sale and rental of housing.

The Foundation has supported two organizations, the National Committee Against Discrimination in Housing (NCDH) and
National Neighbors, that help local constituent groups promote
open housing. NCDH is concerned with opening up housing opportunities for minorities in areas from which they have been
excluded. National Neighbors serves neighborhoods already ra-
cially mixed but threatened with economic and social disruption
because of rapid change. A third national organization, the
Potomac Institute, has received Foundation support for studies of
the racial impact of urban development policies. Grants have also
been made for metropolitan and regional open housing programs
and recently for a few local neighborhood stabilization demonstra-

tions. The Foundation's cumulative commitment to open housing comes to $8.8 million.

CASE 12.   SCHOOL FINANCE REFORM: LATECOMERS

Since 1969, the Ford Foundation has granted $14 million to support research, training, advocacy, and litigation in the reform of public-school financing patterns.[74] In hindsight it appears remarkable that the subject, which is now one of the major activities of the Education and Research Division, took so long to reach our educational agenda. In virtually ignoring the fiscal roots of the education forest we had plenty of company; the subject had hardly been considered in other than the most peripheral manifestations, e.g., citizen rejections of school budgets.[75] The impetus for our entry into the field came from proposals made by the National Urban Coalition and Syracuse University.

The Foundation's rationale for working on the economics and financing of public education is that the traditional pattern for financing schools through property taxes makes the accident of where children live the major determinant of the kind of education they will receive. Within a given state, school districts have enormous differences in taxable wealth per pupil, tax rates for education, and spending per pupil. For seventy-five years or more this basic inequality has existed despite superficial and largely unsuccessful attempts to redress it through state "equalization" formulas.

The underlying theme of the Foundation's education program has been to open improved opportunities for high-quality education, especially to the poor and to minority groups. Because traditional school finance inequalities severely restrict that access by

---

[74]*Paying for Schools and Colleges* (New York: Ford Foundaton, 1976).

[75]Strictly speaking, we did not ignore the economics of education altogether, since we partially supported Theodore Schultz's pioneering work at the University of Chicago on how education contributes to economic growth and distribution of income. His focus, however, was on matters quite distant from the mechanics and equity issues of state financing of public education.

disadvantaged groups, it is right that we assist those seeking to reform them. But we are not trying to sell a single formula to states and localities for the reform of taxation and the distribution of tax funds to schools. (Exactly equal expenditures for the education of every child in a state would probably not provide either equality or fairness.) Our program has been designed to make certain that many more equitable finance systems are devised and that these alternatives are given full consideration by tax or fiscal experts, legislators, and citizens.

Two principal strategies have guided our efforts. The first has been to support long-range efforts to build greater intellectual strength into the reform movement. Changing conditions in school finance have created a demand for a new breed of school finance expert. Governments, research organizations, and universities are searching for persons able to deal with the fiscal and political complexities of the subject.

Approximately half of our funds in school finance have therefore been focused on research and training needs. Major grantees have included the University of California (Berkeley), the Maxwell School at Syracuse University, Teachers College (Columbia University), the University of Chicago, and Stanford University. The university programs are directed by professors who are already intellectual leaders concerned with policy reform in the contemporary school finance field. Each program has involved doctoral students not only in advanced training in public finance and political science, but also in applied research, as interns or research assistants in actual state school finance reform studies.

Our second strategy has been to assist in the development of national resource bases to aid the different reform activities. For example, support has been given to the Lawyers' Committee for Civil Rights Under Law, a group that has provided technical assistance and legal analyses in nearly all of the significant court cases in school finance. A second grant of this type went to the National Urban Coalition, whose school finance projects in five states have helped train and involve minorities in all aspects of the education finance reform movement. We have also assisted the League of

Woman Voters in focusing its considerable energies on school finance, particularly in four states selected by the league. Other grants have been made to the Education Law Center, a public-interest law firm specializing in education problems in New Jersey and Pennsylvania; the Massachusetts Advocacy Center; and the National Conference of State Legislatures (part of the Council of State Governments). In a few cases, we have directly assisted a state-initiated commission or project studying school finance reform.

Throughout these efforts we have attempted to develop a comprehensive program to grapple with the system of school finance rather than simply to group disparate projects under a school finance reform rubric. We have assisted persons holding a variety of views—philosophically and politically—about the desired outcomes of school finance reform so long as these persons share our discomfort with structurally inequitable and discriminatory finance systems. We realize that each state's fiscal system is unique and that no simple solution can be applied across the board. We have also avoided supporting only a single solution out of a decent respect for the proper relation between a private philanthropy and a sensitive public-policy area.

In all of this activity we have had some notable successes and failures. Partly as a result of the Foundation's efforts, other funding organizations, both private and governmental, have seriously entered the field, particularly Carnegie Corporation and the National Institute of Education. Ford and Carnegie grants to the National Urban Coalition have helped attract minority people to this field. Many important school finance reform projects are jointly funded by two or more outside funding sources and increasingly by the grantee's own funds.

Substantial legislative reform of school finance—and, in most cases, a related tax reform—has occurred in perhaps a dozen states. In another two dozen states, badly needed reform has not yet occurred, although in perhaps half of these the necessary organizational and intellectual preconditions for reform exist. In the remaining states, the school financing system does not display the kind of structural inequity that can be changed through state action. Litigators partially supported with our funds have helped to win perhaps ten significant state school finance cases on state constitutional grounds, and in the process they have attracted considerable legislative and media attention not previously focused on school financing questions.

To sum up, we set out with a concern about a particular manifestation of social and racial inequity. We have tried to create broader public and governmental awareness of the seriousness of this inequity, to build the institutional elements for a general reform movement, and to support research and training that can bring new sophistication to the field. At the heart of all these activities, we have tried to legitimize a new perception of the issue and stimulate new ideas about strategies of reform.

CASE 13. EUROPEAN MANAGEMENT EDUCATION: TRANSPLANTING EXPERIENCE

In 1967 the Foundation embarked on a comprehensive program to strengthen management education in Europe. Approximately $9 million was granted for the effort over a six-year period.

We moved into this field because of the widely recognized educational and managerial gap between the United States and Europe and because Europeans themselves wanted to develop business schools that would provide professional training and generate a body of research applicable to their setting. The Foundation was particularly qualified to help because of our earlier program (1955–1965) in helping to improve the level of teaching and research in business schools in the United States. This experience left us with a fairly broad knowledge of the forms and problems of business education and with a wide reputation for trustworthy judgment in the field. The legacy enabled a rather modestly funded program in Europe to go a long way.

The objectives of our management education program in Western Europe stressed the development of teaching and research capabilities that would enable Europe's management education systems to grow on their own. We aimed, therefore, (1) to develop a sizable group of trained Europeans who could teach and do research, (2) to establish several high-quality graduate and professional institutions, and (3) to develop an international but European-based network for advancing research and training in this field.

Some $2.2 million was spent on a large doctoral fellowship program for young European scholars. This program was the primary instrument for the development of a cadre of well-trained European teachers and researchers. Each person chosen was given a three-year fellowship to study for a doctorate at a leading American business school.

Approximately $4.8 million was spent to foster the creation of new centers of professional training and research in management education and to improve existing centers. In partnership with several European governments, the Foundation helped establish (with a grant of $1 million) the European Institute for Advanced Study in Management, in Brussels. The institute's role was to encourage doctoral-level business research in Europe and, through its network of participating faculty members, to assist the exchange of research findings.

An example of building on an existing institutional base was our $1 million matching support for the European Institute of Business Administration (INSEAD) in France. Established in the late 1950s, INSEAD had an effective but not particularly innovative or research-oriented training program. In the early 1970s, however, the institute developed plans to stress research and to strengthen its financial base and outreach, and our funds helped it achieve these objectives.

Finally, a European Foundation for Management Development (Belgium), which was established in 1971 with our support, serves as a useful communications network. It represents national institutions, academic centers, and individuals engaged in management development.

We also supported specific research projects for a total of $1.1

million. In selecting projects we considered not only the importance of the problems to be investigated but also the extent to which the grant might assist the development of the sponsoring institution.

Interesting complements to our work in Western Europe were a series of exchange programs with Hungary, Poland, and Rumania and periodic seminars on management education topics with Soviet scholars and planners. In the exchanges, young scholars from Eastern Europe spent up to a year in American business schools, while selected American educators visited Eastern Europe to teach and conduct research. The USSR/U.S. seminars, held on a rotating basis annually here and in the Soviet Union, consisted of week-long workshops followed by visits to corporations and planning agencies. A jointly authored book is likely to emerge from these efforts.

The Foundation terminated the European management education program when it appeared that we had fulfilled our objectives. The management gap was not closed, but we were persuaded that the European management education movement had become self-sustaining and that a gradual reduction of our support would not retard the movement. The decision was a calculated risk, but in retrospect it was correct. In virtually every major European country there now is strong management education, and most of our grants have left a durable legacy. The European Institute continues without our support, and the Europeans who studied in the United States under Foundation fellowships are now part of the well-trained group of scholars. Although not all of our research grants turned out to meet the high expectations we had for them, the batting average seems respectable.

In sum, it appears that the overall program objectives were well chosen, timely, and represented a happy meshing of European interests and priorities with the Foundation's capacity to help. Clearly, the key element in all of this work was the quality of the European commitment and ability to follow through. Instances where efforts fell far short of expectations represented our having chosen inadequate European partners—inadequate either because the country's general commitment to the program faltered or because the specific individuals turned out not to be up to the tasks. The notably successful ventures, on the other hand, were those where we managed to find individuals who commanded the respect of their countrymen and who enjoyed the full backing of their governments.

CASE 14.   INTERNATIONAL LANGUAGE PROGRAMS: REFLECTIONS OF DEVELOPMENT VIEWS

The Foundation has been concerned with the complex language problems of the developing nations since it began programs of international assistance in the early 1950s. Some $23 million has been granted in this field.[76]

The background of our work was the emergent nationalism in the Third World after World War II and the determined drive of the new countries toward independence and modernization. Among the consequences of this drive was the need to establish effective communication with advanced industrial societies through one or more of their languages (e.g., English, French, Russian). At the same time, newly independent nations had to resolve internal problems of communication stemming from the coexistence of several languages within their borders.

For about a decade, beginning in 1952, the Foundation concentrated on the first of these problems through programs to teach English as a second language (ESL). Our work in ESL had two major components. One was to assist efforts within countries (Indonesia, Egypt, India) to strengthen the resources for teaching

[76]This brief case study is limited to language programs abroad. In the last ten years, however, the Foundation has also addressed the problems of multilingualism within the United States, where speakers of foreign languages or nonstandard varieties of English face some of the same difficulties as do linguistic minority groups in other societies. Foundation-supported programs in the United States have focused mainly on the relation between language and learning among minorities. It is worth noting that domestic and international staff members increasingly have cooperated in shaping an overall strategy on support of language programs.

English; the other was to help develop ESL programs in universities in the United States.

The stress on ESL reflected the view that developing countries would move through a series of changes toward modernity as the West knows it if they were aided by the kind of education Western nations could provide. Since the necessary knowledge was generally available in English, it seemed reasonable that knowledge of English be increased.

By 1960 these views had changed greatly, as we were placing increasing emphasis on the role of local or regional languages in national development. Patterns of development in different countries were far more diverse than we and most others had suspected, and we came to appreciate more fully that language is central to group identity and that linguistic diversity symbolizes the self-determination of peoples as perhaps nothing else does. In this new phase the Foundation began supporting institutions in the developing countries and research by scholars in the United States aimed at creating effective bilingual or multilingual educational programs.

Six basic kinds of activity, combined in various ways, have made up the Foundation's language projects and programs:

1. Basic and applied research, including surveys of language use and studies of ways in which language facilitates or retards personal and group development
2. Institution-building
3. Training of research scholars, language educators, and advanced specialists in language teaching (both abroad and domestically)
4. Preparation and production of instructional materials, and provision of teaching equipment
5. In-service and preservice training of classroom teachers (usually within their own country)
6. Strengthening organization and communication through support of associations, journals, and specialized conferences and workshops

During the 1950s most of our grants were ad hoc largely because there was little long-term planning for language teaching in the developing countries. Many countries in which we had language programs (Indonesia, Egypt, Kenya, Nigeria, India) pressed us to establish or to strengthen resources for teaching ESL. Most of our projects, however, tended to be marginal to the main educational stream: ESL training for civil servants and the preparation of radio programs for schools (Nigeria); writing of textbooks for a junior college (Turkey); language laboratories (Peru, Iraq, Syria, Egypt, Nigeria). In a number of cases the Foundation picked up where the United States government or the Rockefeller Foundation had left off (the Philippines, Tunisia, Egypt).

With the funding of the Central Institute of English in India in 1958, the Foundation began supporting projects that linked language study, including ESL, to the development of various countries' educational systems. These changes were perhaps most significantly marked by the Foundation's establishment of the Center for Applied Linguistics (CAL) in the United States in 1959.

The Foundation was heavily involved with CAL throughout the 1960s, supporting it with grants totaling $6.7 million. Created as a clearinghouse, catalyst, and coordinator, CAL encouraged greater cooperation among universities, foundations, and government agencies concerned with language problems. It became a link, for example, between linguists specializing in critically important unfamiliar languages and those working on the teaching of ESL. Perhaps most important, CAL gradually helped put into effect a major conclusion drawn from the experience of the 1950s: teaching ESL in any country should be undertaken only within the context of the country's total linguistic, educational, and cultural background. As obvious as this now seems, it was a relatively novel doctrine in the 1960s.

In the later phase of our language activities abroad, the Foundation has assisted a variety of efforts to relate education to linguistic diversity. For example, we helped establish in the Philippines the Language Study Center (LSC) in 1962. Specializing in problems of bilingualism, LSC's program of research and training aims to provide instruction in English and Pilipino (originally called Tagalog) to students at all levels of the educational system.

New support for research during this period was directed principally to sociolinguistic surveys. In order to plan language programs, especially in education, it is necessary to learn the answers to the multiple question, Who speaks (or writes) what language to whom, when, and to what end? The most ambitious survey we supported was conducted in five East African countries (Tanzania, Uganda, Kenya, Ethiopia, and Zambia). Other smaller but also useful surveys were conducted in the Philippines and in Jordan. Related research has focused on what is called language planning, efforts to determine how particular languages or vocabularies should be used for specified purposes. For example, what languages are best suited for scientific or medical training? For everyday commerce? For newspapers or radio broadcasts? And which languages should be taught schoolchildren in what sequence in multilingual societies?

A final point: the Foundation has for more than twenty years acted with remarkable persistence on a conviction of the importance of language in the development process, despite the shifting emphases of our programs. Yet, although events seem to have proved our conviction to be correct, we continue to stand pretty much alone as a private aid agency working in language programs. The sustained interest and conviction of Melvin Fox and Francis Sutton have succeeded in persuading many doubters in the Foundation, but we have so far not succeeded in persuading other foundations to join us. It may be that other aid agencies are bemused by the subject, as many of us have been from time to time. It all seems too technical, too abstruse, and that may be because to many, the subject of linguistics is associated with the work of specialists like Noam Chomsky, whose highly theoretical, even philosophical, approach intimidates even the educated laity. Yet, it may be said with some confidence that despite their shortcomings, our overseas language programs have dealt with inescapable, real problems and have often led the way in developing practical means to solve them.[77] Scholars seem to be listening, and so are the officials and administrators in the developing countries. Why so many others continue to turn a deaf ear remains a puzzle.

CASE 15.   CIVIL RIGHTS LITIGATION: WELLSPRING OF JUDICIAL HISTORY

Most support for the civil rights movement from private sources—whether foundations, corporations, or individuals—has gone to research, scholarships, and the strengthening of institutions weakened by discrimination. Litigation as an instrument of civil rights reform has received a relatively small share of the total.

The earlier reluctance of philanthropic institutions to support litigation on behalf of civil rights may have been rooted in part in the traditional view of the judicial function. This holds that where there is an injustice that the courts can correct, the victims will inevitably come forward to present their case. Yet, in reality, plaintiffs often are reluctant to take such action. Among other reasons, they may lack the money to initiate a suit and carry it through in the courts.

Another reason for philanthropic hesitation has been the worry that providing funds for the conduct of litigation might, regardless of the merits of the case, be an inappropriate intrusion into the judicial process. Eventually it was established in the courts that group advocacy of individual rights is permissible. But even then, there was no outpouring of philanthropic aid.

In our case these were not the principal inhibitions. Our delay stemmed from the fact that until 1967 we gave very little support to civil rights work at all. Then, in the latter 1960s, our domestic priorities shifted to focus on programs for disadvantaged minorities. This decisive change was reflected in a rapid increase in grants related to minority rights, from only 2.5 percent of our annual giving in 1960 to 38.5 percent in 1968 and 40 percent in 1970.

[77]For a fuller analysis of the Foundation's language programs abroad, see Melvin J. Fox, *Language and Development: A Retrospective Survey 1952–1974* (New York: Ford Foundation, 1975).

But only a part of this money was for litigation. Ranked in the order of dollar support allocated to minorities and the poor are four areas of Foundation action:

1. Community development, particularly in inner-city ghettos
2. Civil rights advocacy by groups such as the Urban League and the NAACP (as a separate entity, distinct from the NAACP Legal Defense and Educational Fund)
3. Civil rights litigation
4. Public-interest law

This scale of priorities reflected the efforts of other institutions. In some cases—community development, for example—our work complemented considerable support from public and other private sources. Civil rights groups also received substantial assistance from other private groups and individuals. Not so with civil rights litigation, however. (Public-interest law was a new field when we entered it and has only gradually built up some diversity of assistance.)

Our grants for civil rights litigation, totaling some $18 million, reflect the following objectives: to help remove barriers to equality caused by discrimination on the basis of race, ethnic background, or sex; to help provide equal access for minorities and the poor to housing, education, jobs, and other avenues to opportunity; and to help ensure fair treatment by government.

Our first grants in the field, in 1967, were to the NAACP Legal Defense and Educational Fund, which had a solid reputation for competence, and to the Lawyers' Committee for Civil Rights Under Law, which grew out of a 1963 White House meeting between President Kennedy and a group of prominent lawyers who were concerned about the nation's persistent problems of political, economic, and social inequity. The bulk of our grants to the Lawyers' Committee went to support of its office in Mississippi, where it was an important presence because of the extent of civil rights litigation in the South at the height of the civil rights movement.

Subsequently, we broadened our support of civil rights litigation to include seven other organizations, four of which we helped establish to concentrate on special problems of particular groups: the Native American Rights Fund (NARF); the Mexican-American Legal Defense and Educational Fund (MALDEF), the Puerto Rican Legal Defense and Education Fund, and the Women's Law Fund. The other three, which work on various substantive issues, are the National Committee Against Discrimination in Housing; the Legal Action Center, concerned mainly with litigation on behalf of former addicts and ex-offenders; and the Center for National Policy Review, which monitors civil rights and equal-opportunity legislation and policy by federal government agencies.

During the period of our support these organizations have brought to court and won some of the most significant civil rights cases in judicial history. They have contributed to major progress toward equalizing municipal services in black and white neighborhoods; to a series of equal-employment decisions on behalf of Spanish-speaking Americans, blacks, women, and ex-offenders; to the restoration of important rights and resources to several Indian tribes; to mandated bilingual instruction for Spanish-speaking students; and to protection of rights in access to housing and in law enforcement.

Our support did not spell the difference between life and death for more established groups like the NAACP Legal Defense and Educational Fund. Yet, for the newer organizations like MALDEF and NARF, our support was crucial.

CASE 16. SOCIAL SCIENCE DEVELOPMENT IN LATIN AMERICA: SELF-RELIANCE FOR PROGRESS

Latin America was the last of the major developing regions to receive Foundation attention. We created a separate Latin America office in New York in 1959 and opened our first field office in Rio de Janeiro in 1961. From then on, we moved into new programmatic terrain as well. The region had a higher level of development than

Asia, Africa, and the Middle East, and the theories of development and social change that had originated in North America and Europe were increasingly challenged by Latin Americans during the 1960s. Therefore, although we made sizable investments in the first few years in traditional areas (economics, business and public administration, the strengthening of universities, urban and development planning), both the Foundation and the Latins soon felt the need to create competence in other fields. These included analyzing and understanding the historical and social roots of Latin-American societies, developing and testing various solutions for the region's special needs, and establishing closer links both among Latin-American social scientists and with their counterparts in the rest of the world.

By the middle of the decade we had formulated a strategy that included the development of the social sciences as a means of helping Latin-American societies develop self-reliance in understanding and coping with their own problems. To date we have committed some $50 million to social science development in Latin America.[78] Our objectives were (1) to develop basic training and research capacities in key social science disciplines; (2) to stimulate an indigenous tradition of social science research; and (3) to encourage regional and national networks of social scientists for collaborative work on problems of mutual interest, particularly agriculture and rural development, education, population, and the analysis and testing of development strategies.

Recent trends in Latin America have favored the noneconomic social sciences, which were relatively neglected in the early years, and interdisciplinary research on such problems as population, education, rural development, and nutrition. And in contrast to the pattern of the early 1960s, assistance over the past decade has been almost wholly channeled directly to Latin America, rather than through North American intermediaries.

---

[78]Funds have been allocated as follows: $14.1 million for agricultural economics and the social science aspects of rural development; $13.3 million for general economics and related policy analysis; and $22 million for other social science development.

Most of our grants have been to Latin-American institutions, public and private universities, private research centers, and selected regional bodies. Grants to governments have been less frequent and generally have been targeted to specific training or policy analysis objectives. The institutions have used our funds to train staff, develop curricula, recruit high-quality students, establish research and publication programs, and strengthen libraries and other supporting facilities needed for advanced work in social science, typically master's-degree level. We have made conscious efforts to develop a few "centers of excellence" to serve as models for development elsewhere and as sources of trained faculty. Over time, grants to the stronger institutions have shifted from institution-building objectives to emphasize research, policy analysis, encouragement of links with other institutions and groups, and related efforts to apply the skills developed. Recently, general, or core, support for a number of the best centers has been terminated through a series of long-term "tie-off" grants, including several endowments. Future grants to these institutions, if any, will be directed to bringing their capabilities to bear on problems of particular interest to the Foundation.

Grants to individuals have supplemented institutional grants in several important ways. For example, they have been used for advanced training of staff and professional development through travel and study. Through the Graduate Fellowship program and the special Agricultural Economics program in Argentina, the regional pool of highly trained social scientists has been expanded with beneficial, if not always entirely predictable, results for the work of the institutions and scholarly networks we have supported. Individual grant programs have also played a key role in providing support for individual research in countries where institutional bases are weak or nonexistent. Finally, assistance to individuals and groups has been an integral part of our efforts to help social science communities that are being threatened or destroyed by political repression, as in Chile, for example.

Increasingly, our grants have aimed at fostering professional collaboration on selected problems by teams of researchers across national and regional lines. For example, we have helped such professional groups as the Brazilian Economics Association and the Latin-American Council for the Social Sciences to establish and coordinate joint research and training projects. Ad hoc research teams, drawing on talent from a number of sources, have been supported for work on such topics as the economics of water management, rural development, and nonformal education. Still another means of advancing collaborative work has been support of more organized research consortia, such as ECIEL, a regional research program on economic integration. Special efforts have been made to encourage mutual support and respect between Latin-American scholars and those in developed countries. A principal example is the work of the Joint Committee on Latin-American Studies of the U.S. Social Science Research Council, which derives the largest part of its funding from the Foundation.

In recent years, unfortunately, we have felt increasingly obliged to make another kind of social science grant—one aimed at bolstering institutions or rescuing individuals in highly repressive or unstable environments. The situations of Argentina in 1966, Brazil in 1969, and the Southern Cone (Chile, Argentina, Uruguay, and Paraguay) after 1973 have led the Foundation to try to protect and sustain portions of the intellectual communities of countries in which human rights and intellectual freedom, in our judgment, are adversely affected. The Foundation's efforts have been of two kinds: (1) assistance to help relocate selected individuals, many of them trained by the Foundation, who have been forced to leave their home countries and pursue their careers elsewhere; and (2) research support to those who are able to continue working at home but who need both the resources and protection afforded by Foundation assistance to function with relative independence. Our current activity in the Southern Cone is predominantly of the latter character.

Throughout most of the 1960s and even now, the Foundation has stood relatively alone among external funding agencies in the willingness to support institutional development in the social sciences. However, as the number of trained Latin-American social scientists has increased, as institutions have become stronger, and as graduate training and research programs have begun to bear fruit in at least some areas, additional sources of funding have become available, especially for research. Although few agencies are prepared to give general support even to such a highly competent and innovative institution as the Center for Planning in Chile, for example, several now seem interested in supporting particular projects of the center, among them research on poverty, employment, income distribution, and comparative national development models. Even in such situations, however, Foundation assistance, usually on a smaller scale, frequently helps to assure minimum institutional stability and to fill research gaps.

Quantitatively, the results of the Foundation's social science program in Latin America are substantial, whether measured in numbers of graduate programs, in numbers of individuals with advanced training in the social sciences, in the range of disciplines that are now fairly strong, in the volume and scope of research and publications, or in terms of the interaction of Latin-American social scientists among themselves and with their peers around the world. In contrast to the relatively barren scene of scarcely fifteen years ago, Latin-American social science today is vigorous and still growing, and we have played an important role in bringing about the change.

Qualitatively, the reviews are somewhat more mixed. Some of the graduate programs are of good-to-excellent quality, and a few are able to conduct first-rate doctoral training programs. Others are uneven, and a few have slipped back after promising beginnings. A few have been virtually destroyed as a result of political events. The research produced by the Latin-American social science community also shows substantial variations in quality. Some of it is among the best anywhere, both in methodological standards and in originality. Some of it, however, is pedestrian, irrelevant, or simply bad. Generally, however, progress to date has been remarkable, and there is every reason to expect it to continue.

Finally, on the question of whether our large-scale development of the social sciences is likely in the long run to help Latin-

American societies solve their problems, we can make only modest claims. Early United States development assistance, including the Foundation's, tended to be based on blind faith in modern social science techniques, especially the quantitative, and in the possibilities of social engineering. But Latin-American social scientists, by and large, never fully accepted such notions. They have continued to look to Europe, and increasingly to their own work, for a new kind of synthesis, a blend of modern, empirical social science and their own inherited classic, humanistic traditions. The results to date, predictably, have been somewhat confused and uncertain. The insights and greater competence emerging from the social sciences, however, are playing a key role in helping Latin-American societies achieve a true understanding of themselves and thus give them a chance to gain greater control over their destinies.

Appendix

A Selected Chronology of the Ford Foundation

1936

Ford Foundation is established and chartered in Michigan by Henry Ford and his son Edsel Ford with an initial gift of $25,000.

Edsel Ford becomes president of the Foundation.

1936–1950

Grants are confined almost entirely to Michigan philanthropies of interest to the Ford family, mainly the Henry Ford Hospital and the Edison Institute.

1937

Henry and Edsel Ford each donate to the Foundation 125,000 shares of nonvoting stock in Ford Motor Company.

1943

Edsel Ford dies. Henry Ford II, his son, assumes office as Foundation president.

1947

The elder Henry Ford dies.

1948

Trustees appoint a study committee of independent consultants under the chairmanship of H. Rowan Gaither, Jr., a San Francisco lawyer, to chart the reorganization of the Foundation into a national organization.

Foundation receives 1,153,809 shares of class "A" nonvoting stock from the estate of Edsel Ford.

1950

Amendment of the Articles of Incorporation formally separates the Foundation from Ford family control.

Henry Ford II resigns as president of the Foundation to become chairman of the board of trustees. Paul G. Hoffman, former businessman and leader of the Marshall Plan, becomes president.

Foundation receives 26,099 shares of class "A" nonvoting stock from estate of Henry Ford.

Gaither committee presents report to the trustees, setting forth five broad areas of Foundation action. The corresponding grant programs that emerged in the early 1950s are given in parentheses:

1. The establishment of peace (Overseas Development, International Training and Research, International Affairs)
2. The strengthening of democracy (Public Affairs)
3. The strengthening of the economy (Economic Development and Administration)
4. Education in a democratic society (Education)
5. Individual behavior and human relations (Behavioral Sciences)

Henry Ford Hospital receives $13.6 million-grant for construction of a diagnostic clinic building.

Funds are appropriated for Overseas Development program in South and Southeast Asia and the Middle East.

1951

Four associate directors of the Foundation are appointed: Robert M. Hutchins, chancellor of the University of Chicago (later, president of the Fund for the Republic); Milton Katz, a former Marshall Plan ambassador in Europe; Chester A. Davis, an agricultural specialist from government; and H. Rowan Gaither, Jr.

Foundation headquarters are established in Pasadena, California, for planning and directing program activities, with New York office receiving grant applications and Detroit office handling fiscal management.

Three independent funds are established by the Foundation:
1. The Fund for the Advancement of Education (which then receives $71.5 million in grants between 1951 and 1967)
2. The Fund for Adult Education ($47.4 million between 1951 and 1961, when it ceases operations)
3. The East European Fund ($3.8 million between 1951 and 1954)

Radio and Television Workshop is set up to improve the cultural use of television and radio on commercial networks (1951–1956, $3 million).

1952

Fund for the Republic is established with an appropriation of $15 million to concentrate on problems of civil liberties in the United States.

Select Committee of the House of Representatives, led by Representative Eugene Cox, investigates alleged subversive or Communist-influenced activities among foundations.

Resources for the Future is established as an independent corporation to improve the development, conservation, and use of natural resources through programs of research and education ($44.6 million, 1952–1977).

Foreign Area Fellowship program to promote research and study on Asia and the Near East begins.

Educational Television and Radio Center (renamed the National Educational Television and Radio Center in 1959) is established by the Fund for Adult Education.

Intercultural Publications is set up as an independent fund to advance appreciation of differing cultures through the exchange of ideas and literary and artistic productions.

"Omnibus" is produced by the Radio and Television Workshop.

U.N. High Commissioner for Refugees is granted $2.9 million to assist refugees in Western Europe.

1953

Paul G. Hoffman resigns as president and is succeeded by H. Rowan Gaither, Jr.

Pasadena office closes and headquarters are consolidated in New York City.

Economic Development and Administration program is established.

Representative B. Carroll Reece initiates second investigation of foundations as follow-up to Cox committee investigation of 1952.

1954

Center for Advanced Study in the Behavioral Sciences is established at Stanford, California, with $3.4-million grant.

Population Council receives first Foundation grant for research on world population problems ($94.4 million, 1954–1977).

1955

Center for International Legal Studies is established at Harvard University with an appropriation of $2 million.

National Merit Scholarships are established jointly with Carnegie Corporation, with initial grant of $20 million given by the Foundation (grants in subsequent years will bring total Foundation support to $38.5 million).

Foundation takes first step to diversify its financial holdings by announcing public sale of Ford Motor Company stock. Sale takes place in 1956, and yields $641 million.

Announcement of large block of grant giving from anticipated proceeds of stock sale (grants are actually made in 1956):

1. $260 million to more than 600 private four-year colleges and universities to increase faculty salaries.
2. $198 million to 3,500 voluntary, nonprofit hospitals to improve and extend their services
3. $90 million to 44 privately supported medical schools

Foundation appropriates $15 million for a program in mental health.

Major effort to strengthen business education in the United States is initiated (concluded 1965, $46.3 million).

Youth Development program begins (1955–1968, $12.5 million).

1956

H. Rowan Gaither, Jr., resigns as president and becomes chairman of the board of trustees.

Henry T. Heald is elected president.

Council on Library Resources is established with a grant of $5 million (1956–1977, $31.5 million).

Five-year program to stimulate publication in the humanities and social sciences by university presses begins (program total, $2.8 million).

Program of grants concerning the aged begins. The program will last eight years and total $6.7 million.

Hagerstown, Maryland, receives first in series of grants for experiment using closed-circuit television for instruction in the public schools ($1 million, 1956–1965).

1957

Woodrow Wilson National Fellowship Foundation receives initial grant of $24.5 million (ultimate total, $56.9 million).

Science and Engineering program is established (concludes 1966, $85.5 million).

Humanities and the Arts program is established.

Activities relating to Europe are expanded, including appropriation of $1,150,000 to aid Hungarian refugees.

Lincoln Center for the Performing Arts receives $2.5-million grant. Subsequent grants of $10 million in 1958 and $12.5 million in 1963 will bring total support of $25 million toward helping create the new arts center.

Programs of scholarly and cultural exchanges between the West and Eastern Europe begin.

1958

John J. McCloy, chairman of the board of Chase Manhattan Bank, becomes chairman of the board of the Foundation, succeeding H. Rowan Gaither, Jr.

Grant of $6.2 million is provided for a major ten-year expansion of the Brookings Institution.

Foundation extends Overseas Development program to Africa.

"Continental Classroom," an experiment using commercial television channels to teach university-level academic subjects, begins (1958–1961, $1.7 million).

Educational Facilities Laboratories is established. An independent research organization concerned with more efficient construction and use of school and college facilities, it will receive grants totaling $25.8 million between 1958 and 1977.

Program to improve the education of elementary and secondary school teachers is undertaken ($32 million, 1958–1967).

1959

Center for Applied Linguistics is established with Foundation assistance (support totals $6.7 million as of 1977).

Urban research and training grants to universities are initiated (1959–1975, $36 million).

International Institute for Strategic Studies is established with a grant of $150,000 (1957–1977, $2 million).

United Nations receives $6.2 million for construction of a new international library at its New York headquarters.

Higher Education for Business by Robert A. Gordon and James E. Howell is published. Report sets forth standards and guidelines for modern business school curricula.

An $11.4-million program to strengthen engineering faculties begins.

Foundation-supported study *India's Food Crisis and Steps to Meet It* recommends emergency action to help meet India's food production problems.

Overseas Development program is extended to Latin America and the Caribbean.

1960

Ten-year Comprehensive School Improvement Program in public schools throughout the country begins.

Special Program in Education is started to accelerate the development of selected private universities and colleges as important national and regional centers. Also known as "challenge grants" program, it totals $349 million by 1967.

National series of grants is given for master's degree programs to train students for college teaching ($10.2 million, 1960–1966).

Support of non-Western studies in U.S. universities is expanded ($45 million, 1960–1962).

Foundation gives $6.9 million to help establish the International Rice Research Institute in cooperation with the Rockefeller Foundation and appropriates $10.5 million for projects to increase food production in India.

Great Cities and Gray Areas grants are initiated to address problems of the urban poor ($30.9 million, 1960–1966).

Intensive Agricultural Districts program is initiated to demonstrate the most effective ways of expanding national food production in pilot districts in India.

1961

Trustees set up a committee to conduct a general review of the programs and procedures of the Foundation.

Calcutta Metropolitan Planning Organization is established with a grant of $800,000 to formulate a development plan for Calcutta.

1962

Trustees formulate a framework for the Foundation's activities in the 1960s, published in *The Ford Foundation in the 1960s*, the first comprehensive study since the 1950 study committee report. The report directed the Foundation to concentrate for the next decade upon five broad areas; namely, educational affairs, public and economic affairs, international affairs, and the arts and sciences.

Representative Wright Patman of Texas announces investigation of tax exemptions of charitable foundations by the House Select Committee on Small Business.

Harvard University receives $750,000 grant for the Development Advisory Service, a career overseas advisory service in development economics.

Major operating-support grants for performing arts companies begin. Foundation appropriates $9 million to strengthen resident professional theater companies in the United States.

Appropriation of $5 million is approved to help reduce the birthrate in India through intensified family-planning program.

1963

Foundation purchases property on East 43rd Street in New York City on which to construct its new headquarters.

John F. Kennedy Center for the Performing Arts, in Washington, D.C., receives $5 million for construction costs.

Foundation establishes Population program, expanding efforts begun a decade earlier.

Major support for classroom television experimentation is completed (1951–1963, $30.1 million).

Foundation takes steps to strengthen National Educational Television and Radio Center (NET) as a national program service ($90.1 million, 1953–1970).

Appropriation of $2.4 million is approved for the National Defender Project of the National Legal Aid and Defender Association. The project ultimately establishes model programs throughout the country for publicly supported defense of indigent accused persons.

Foundation appropriates $8 million to begin a national program to develop ballet training and performing resources in the United States.

1964

National Achievement Scholarships are established with a grant of $8.1 million, under the aegis of the National Merit Scholarship program, to assist academically promising black students.

Scholarship support totaling $2 million is provided for students at thirty-six independent art schools and conservatories of music.

Midwest University Consortium for International Affairs is established under a grant of $3.5 million (total, $6.2 million, 1964–1976).

1965

Henry T. Heald resigns as president and trustee.

John J. McCloy retires as chairman of the board of trustees.

Resources and the Environment program is established.

Advanced training for journalists is assisted through initial grants totaling $4,475,000 to Columbia University, Harvard University, the Southern Regional Education Board, Stanford University ($7 million, 1965–1969).

Development of international studies programs at U.S. universities is assisted through endowment and operating grants totaling $72 million (1965–1966).

Harvard University receives $1.5 million for construction of the Center of Human Reproduction ($3 million between 1965 and 1969).

Two-million-dollar grant is made to help establish the John F. Kennedy Institute of Politics at Harvard University.

Foundation initiates program of matching funds for community-supported educational television stations.

Ten-year $80-million series of endowment and operating support grants to symphony orchestras is authorized.

1966

McGeorge Bundy becomes president.

Julius A. Stratton, president of the Massachusetts Institute of Technology, assumes office as chairman of the board of trustees.

International Legal Center is established with $3-million grant to stimulate study of the role of law in international relations and in the development of new nations.

Plan for model communications satellite system, including benefits for public broadcasting, is submitted to the Federal Communications Commission.

International Maize and Wheat Improvement Center is established jointly, with Rockefeller Foundation and support of the Mexican government ($11.8 million, 1966–1977).

Leadership Development Program is initiated to provide opportunities for promising rural educators and community leaders ($11.5 million, 1966–1975).

The Brookings Institution receives a $14-million grant for general support ($36 million, 1954–1977).

1967

Foundation moves to new headquarters at 320 East 43rd Street, New York, N.Y.

Controversy arises over the Foundation's role in New York City school decentralization.

Seven-year, $41.5-million program is launched to improve the efficiency of graduate education in humanities and social sciences.

Six-year, $9-million program to strengthen management education in Europe begins.

Foundation expands support of civil rights with major grants to NAACP Special Contribution Fund, the National Urban League, and the Southern Christian Leadership Conference.

Public Broadcast Laboratory receives $10 million.

NAACP Legal Defense and Educational Fund receives $1-million grant to create and operate a national office for the rights of the indigent.

1968

Foundation helps establish the Urban Institute with a grant of $1 million.

Initial program-related investments made under $10-million authorization (total authorization: $50 million, 1968–1977).

Fund for the City of New York is established with $1.1-million grant in recognition of the Foundation's full tax exemption on its land and building.

Mexican-American Legal Defense and Educational Fund is established under a $2.2-million grant.

Series of grants for local public television station development begins ($32 million, 1968–1974).

Council on Legal Education for Professional Responsibility is established under appropriation of $5.4 million.

In cooperation with Corporation for Public Broadcasting, Foundation provides support for national public television programming at major production centers (1970–1977, $81.7 million).

1969

House Ways and Means Committee begins hearings on tax reform. Resulting Tax Reform Act imposes an excise tax on foundations' net investment income, and establishes a new tax on foundations for violating certain new prohibitions on foundation activities (e.g., may not make grants to individuals unless they comply with new regulations; voter education activities can be supported only under specific conditions, etc.).

Common Fund for Nonprofit Organizations is established to provide joint investment management of nonprofit college and university endowment funds.

Program of assistance to minority Community Development Corporations begins, including grants to groups in Brooklyn, Los Angeles, and Mississippi ($48 million in grants and $10 million in program-related investments, 1969–1977).

Public Broadcasting Service is established with a grant of $1.2 million as a membership corporation responsible for the scheduling and delivery of programs.

Foundation-sponsored *The Law and the Lore of Endowment Funds,* by William L. Cary and Craig B. Bright, is published.

School finance reform grants begin (1969–1977, $14.4 million).

1970

Upper Division Scholarship program for minority students is established ($7.5 million, 1970–1976).

Venture Fund grants are made to forty-nine colleges to encourage innovation in undergraduate education ($8.5 million, 1970–1974).

Police Foundation is established under a $30-million, five-year appropriation.

Support of public-interest law centers begins (1970–1977, $13 million).

Native American Rights Fund is established under a grant of $115,000 ($2.9 million through 1977).

1971

Institute for Educational Leadership is established with a grant of $410,000.

Cash Reserve program is initiated to attack recurring financial problems of performing arts organizations.

Julius A. Stratton retires as chairman of the board of trustees.

Alexander Heard, chancellor of Vanderbilt University, is elected chairman of the board of trustees.

Foundation commits $100 million for six years to increase minority opportunities in higher education, with half of the funds going for minority graduate fellowships and half going for institutional development at selected private black colleges. (Institutional support for black colleges: $37 million, 1960–1971; graduate fellowships for minorities: $12 million, 1967–1971.)

1972

Drug Abuse Council is established jointly with Carnegie Corporation, the Commonwealth Fund, and the Henry J. Kaiser Foundation ($8.8 million, 1972–1976).

Committee on Public Policy and Social Organization is established.

Cable Television Information Center is established with a $2.5-million grant ($2.8 million, 1972–1976).

Energy Policy Project is established to conduct research and analysis of the nation's energy problems ($4.15 million, 1972–1975). Final report, *A Time to Choose: America's Energy Future*, is published in 1974.

Women's programs begin with formation of internal task force to examine how the Foundation's funds could best be used to advance the status of women.

1973

Foundation announces a final four-year $40-million commitment to public broadcasting (support will total $292 million by the end of 1977).

Foundation commits $75 million, expected to yield $100 million over ten years, to Henry Ford Hospital for major expansion program of medical education and research.

A Foundation Goes to School reports on the successes and failures of the Foundation's $30-million ten-year Comprehensive School Improvement Program.

Foundation commits $1 million for research on subjects identified by C. Fred Bergsten in his report, *The Future of the International Economic Order* ($3.3 million, 1973–1977).

1974

Foundation completes disposition of its holdings of Ford Motor Company stock.

Supported-work demonstration projects are initiated to provide jobs for hard-to-employ people ($5 million as of 1977).

Two-volume study, *The Finances of the Performing Arts: A Ford Foundation Report,* a survey of 166 professional nonprofit theater, opera, ballet, and modern dance companies and symphony orchestras, is published.

Seminars and other activities concerning conflict between the media and the law begin ($817,000 as of 1977).

1975

Major retrenchment program is undertaken owing to declines in the stock market and to remaining commitments under large-scale grant-making in the 1960s and early 1970s. Aim is 50 percent reduction of staff and grants over three-year period. (Previous cutbacks in expenditures occurred in 1967, 1971, and 1974).

Resources for the Future is granted $12 million to conduct public-policy research on energy and the environment.

Expanded program in defense of human rights and intellectual freedom is initiated.

1976

Henry Ford II resigns from the Foundation's board of trustees.

Major review, *Reproduction and Human Welfare: A Challenge to Research*, is completed on the state of reproductive and contraceptive knowledge (total funding of this field, $110 million, 1959 through 1977).

Program of subsidies for the production of new American plays begins ($940,000, 1976 and 1977).

Study of public-policy issues related to development of nuclear power is commissioned. Conducted by a group of twenty-one prominent scientists and scholars, the study will produce the report, *Nuclear Power Issues and Choices* (1977).

International Food Policy Research Institute is established to identify opportunities for increased world food production ($430,000 through 1977).

Trustees review the Foundation's programs and consider program priorities for the 1980s.

1977

Study of welfare policy issues, sponsored jointly with Duke University, is completed.

Harvard University receives $4 million to establish a permanent endowment for arms control study and training.

Program of activities analyzing the wide-ranging impact of organized crime is announced.

Trustees name committee to assist in search for a new president to succeed McGeorge Bundy, who is to retire in 1979.

Foundation announces program of research on the nature of the office of the President of the United States.

Nationwide competition is announced to improve states' role in protecting and managing the environment ($775,000).

FIELDS OF FOUNDATION ACTIVITY

1. *Higher Education (General)—*$1.1 billion
   Objectives:
   Improvement of governance and management
   Strengthening the financial base
   Recruiting and training talented faculty
   Improving faculty salaries and benefits
   Strengthening undergraduate curricula and methods
   Widening access to higher education, particularly for the
      poor, women, and minorities
   Selected Major Actions:

Faculty salary support in private colleges and universities (1956)	$260.0 million
Challenge grants to 84 colleges and universities (1960–70)	349.0 million
Venture Fund grants to 49 colleges for innovation in undergraduate education (1970–74)	8.5 million
Graduate Education program in 10 major research universities (1967–72)	41.5 million
Change magazine (1971–74)	0.9 million
Nontraditional education programs (1970)	4.0 million
Graduate fellowships for minorities (1967–77)	45.2 million
Development of private black colleges (1967–77)	53.3 million
Ethnic studies (1969–72)	7.2 million
Urban research and training in universities (1959–75)	36.0 million

2. *University-Based Programs*
   a. *International Training and Research—*$335.8 million
      Objectives:
      Integrating international studies into graduate and
         professional schools

Strengthening undergraduate teaching of non-Western and international studies

Professionalizing and improving foreign-student exchanges

Promoting scholarly exchanges with the Soviet Union and Eastern Europe

Improving foreign-language teaching

Improving American university cooperation with foreign counterparts

Selected Major Actions:

Support of international studies in American universities (1960–72)	$121.7 million
Foreign Area Fellowship program (1952–77)	35.1 million
Exchanges with the Soviet Union and Eastern Europe (1957–77)	18.2 million
Institute of International Education (1951–77)	7.1 million

b. *Engineering Education*—$71.7 million

Objectives:

Developing "great centers" of engineering research and training

Improving engineering curricula, mainly toward applied science and design

Recruiting and retaining talented faculty

Selected Major Actions:

Massachusetts Institute of Technology (1959)	$9.3 million
Case Institute of Technology (1959–61)	9.0 million
Illinois Institute of Technology (1964)	5.0 million
Stanford University (1959–61)	4.8 million
Cornell University (1961)	4.4 million
Forgivable loan program (1961–65)	7.4 million

c. *Humanistic Scholarship*—$75.4 million

Objectives:

Strengthening research, training, and education in the humanistic disciplines

Improving scholarly resources

Selected Major Actions:

Council on Library Resources (1956–77)	$31.5 million
American Council of Learned Societies postdoctoral fellowships and grants-in-aid (1956–75)	15.3 million
College faculty development (61 colleges) (1968)	2.7 million
University presses program (1956)	2.8 million
Historical papers of the founding fathers (1964)	2.0 million

d. *Business Education*—$55.3 million[1]

Objectives:

Improving leadership of American business

Strengthening the teaching of business administration

Increasing the supply of research-oriented teachers of business

Integrating social sciences, humanities, and mathematical techniques into the business curriculum

Selected Major Actions:

Faculty research and doctoral fellowships (1956–67)	$7.2 million
International Center for Advancement of Management Education (Stanford) (1960)	3.5 million
Institute of Basic Mathematics for Application to Business (Harvard) (1959–62)	0.5 million
European Institute for Advanced Studies in Management, Brussels (1971)	1.0 million

[1]Includes $9 million for European Management Education.

3. *Early Learning and Secondary Education—$389.6 million*[2]

    Objectives:

    Improving teacher education and competence in service

    Improving school administration and educational leader-
    ship

    Improving educational organization and curricula

    Advancing understanding of learning processes

    Developing and expanding preschool education

    Improving public understanding of and participation in
    education

    Reforming educational financing

    Eliminating segregation and advancing minority opportun-
    ity

    Selected Major Actions:

Training educational administrators (1968–77)	$10.3 million
Comprehensive School Improvement program (1960–70)	30.0 million
Teacher education "breakthrough program" (1958–67)	32.0 million
Leadership Development Program (1966–75)	11.5 million
School finance reform (1969–77)	14.4 million
Alternative-school programs (1969–75)	3.4 million
Educational Facilities Laboratories (1958–77)	25.8 million
Decentralization of public school systems (1969–71)	2.0 million

4. *Public Television—$292.3 million*[3]

    Objectives:

[2]Does not include grants for instructional television or the Children's Television Workshop. These grants are listed under 4. *Public Television*. Grants for advancing educational opportunities for women and eliminating sex discrimination are listed under *10. Women's Programs*.

[3]Includes work of the Fund for the Advancement of Education and the Fund for Adult Education.

Assuring reservation of part of the broadcast spectrum for
public television

Demonstrating the possibility of high-level educational and
cultural broadcasting

Developing noncommericial broadcasting throughout the
United States

Developing a public policy in broadcasting

Selected Major Actions:

Construction of educational television stations (1951–63)	$ 4.0 million
Instructional television (1951–60)	11.7 million
Radio and Television Workshop (including "Omnibus") (1951–57)	8.0 million
Released time of faculty for educational television programming (1956–61)	1.8 million
Midwest Program on Airborne Television (1959–62)	14.7 million
National Educational Television and Radio Center (NET) (1953–70)	90.1 million
Public Broadcast Laboratory (1967–69)	12.0 million
New American Television Drama Project (1974–77)	3.0 million
Children's Television Workshop (1971–75)	8.0 million
Station Program Cooperative (1974–77)	12.8 million
Principal production centers (1970–77)	81.7 million
Station Independence program and Public Broadcast Survey Facility (1970–77)	2.3 million
Communication satellite studies (1975–77)	0.7 million
Cable television information (1972–77)	3.1 million

5. *The Arts*—$286.4 million[4]

Objectives:

Developing artistic institutions

Encouraging of innovation in various art fields

[4]Includes grants to the Detroit Museum of Art ($1,920,000), Museum of Modern
Art ($1,000,000), Lincoln Center ($25,000,000), Kennedy Center ($5,000,000).

Discovering and developing individual talent through train-
ing, provision of outlets, and other career opportunities
Widening minority opportunities in and access to the arts
Strengthening the long-term base of support for the arts

Selected Major Actions:

Cash Reserve program (1971–77)	$25.8 million
Symphony Orchestra program (1965)	80.2 million
Dance Theatre of Harlem (1969–76)[5]	3.6 million
Tamarind Lithography Workshop (1960–70)	2.2 million
Development of resident theaters (1962–74)	17.7 million
Development of ballet companies (1963–74)	13.6 million

6. *Government Performance*—$126.7 million[6]

Objectives:

Strengthening the performance of government at all levels
Recruiting and training talented persons for public service
Improving knowledge of government processes and
policies
Widening participation in the political process
Understanding elections and voting behavior
Improving government constitutions and charters
Strengthening political science research and training
Promoting citizen awareness of and access to public policy
Maintaining proportional representation in legislative
bodies
Urban, metropolitan, and regional studies

Selected Major Actions:

Fund for the City of New York (1968–76)	$10.1 million
American Political Science Association (1956–66)	4.1 million
Citizenship Clearing House (1956–61)	3.1 million
Graduate training in public policy (1973)	2.6 million

[5]Includes cash reserve grant ($469,581).
[6]Includes $6.7 million for public-policy grants; does not include urban research and
training programs in universities, listed under 1. *Higher Education (General)*.

Regional Plan Association (1956–77)	2.4 million

7. *Law and the Administration of Justice*—$121.3 million

Objectives:

Improving the courts, correctional agencies, police, and other parts of the justice system

Strengthening law school preparation in criminal law and public service

Improving access to the legal system for the accused and groups otherwise unrepresented

Selected Major Actions:

Police Foundation (1970–77)	$25.9 million
Council on Legal Education for Professional Responsibility (1968–74)	11.0 million
National Legal Aid and Defender Association (1953–72)	7.4 million
National Council on Crime and Delinquency (1955–70)	3.6 million
Vera Institute of Justice (1966–77)	4.3 million

8. *Poverty and the Disadvantaged*—$220.8 million[7]

Objectives:

Expansion of knowledge and understanding of poverty

Supporting demonstrations and experiments in the reduction and elimination of poverty

Monitoring government programs affecting poverty and the disadvantaged

Assisting action programs to ensure fair implementation of public policies to advance the disadvantaged

Eliminating discrimination in housing and other services

Selected Major Actions:

Community Development Corporations (1967–77)	$50.0 million
Gray Areas (1960–67)	26.9 million

---

[7]Does not include support of legal services for the disadvantaged, listed under *7. Law and the Administration of Justice*, or of open housing, or of the larger minority rights organizations such as the National Urban League, listed under *9. Civil Rights, Civil Liberties, Race Relations*.

Housing (exclusive of open housing) (1955–
77)   18.4 million
Professional training of minorities (1963–
77)   15.1 million
Center for Community Change (1969–77)   9.2 million

9. *Civil Rights, Civil Liberties, Race Relations*[8]—$96.0 million

Objectives:
Eliminating discrimination in all walks of American life
Promoting intergroup understanding and relations
Strengthening understanding and protection of civil liber-
ties

Selected Major Actions:
Fund for the Republic (1952–53) $15.0 million
National Urban League (1966–77)   17.8 million
Open housing (1962, 1966–77)   11.3 million
Southern Regional Council (1953–77)   8.6 million
Metropolitan Applied Research Center
(1967–76)   4.7 million
National Association for the Advance-
ment of Colored People Special
Contribution Fund (1967–77)   5.4 million
NAACP Legal Defense and Educational
Fund (1967–76)   3.3 million
Voter Education Project (1970–76)[9]   0.8 million

10. *Women's Programs*—$16.5 million

Objectives:
Eliminating sex discrimination at all educational levels
Promoting economic stability of women
Protecting legal rights of women
Improving the status of women in developing countries

Selected Major Actions:
Faculty and doctoral fellowships for research on women (1972–75) $1.0 million

[8]See note to item 8.
[9]Approximately $370,000 was granted in prior years through the Southern Re-
gional Council.

Technical assistance projects on affirmative action in education (1973–75)	1.0 million
Child care and family support projects (1969–77)	3.3 million
Center for Policy Research on Women (1975)	0.3 million
Beirut University Institute for Women's Studies in the Arab World (1975)	0.2 million

11. *Resources and the Environment*—$92.0 million

Objectives:

Improving the conservation and management of natural resources

Strengthening research and training in the environmental sciences

Supporting constructive citizen action on behalf of the environment

Improving environmental policy in such areas as energy, land use, pollution, and resource scarcity

Strengthening the capacity for analyzing and managing environmental problems

Improving environmental education in elementary schools

Preserving open space and wilderness areas

Selected Major Actions:

Resources for the Future (1953–77)	$47.5 million
International Union for the Conservation of Nature and National Resources (1970–74)	1.0 million
Ecological training and research (1967–70)	9.8 million
Energy Policy Project (1972–75)	4.2 million
Regional Environmental Management Program (1970–74)	3.2 million
Municipal Conservation Commissions (1972–75)	0.7 million
Save the Redwoods League (1965–68)	1.5 million
The Nature Conservancy (1966–73)	1.5 million
Environmental law (1968–78)	7.2 million

Environmental policy analysis (1974–77)   2.7 million

12.   *Economic and Social Research in the United States and Europe—*
$87.6 million[10]

Objectives:
  Improving understanding of economic problems in the
  United States and abroad
  Increasing the number of professionally trained social sci-
  entists
  Strengthening social science research institutions in the
  United States and Europe

Selected Major Actions:
  Brookings Institution (general support)
  (1958–66) $20.2 million
  Doctoral and faculty fellowships (1956–73)   11.5 million
  National Bureau of Economic Research
  (1959)   2.4 million
  Center for Advanced Study in the Be-
  havioral Sciences (1954–69)   17.8 million
  Joint Council on Economic Education
  (1957–66)   2.6 million

13.   *International Affairs*—$121.4 million

Objectives:
  Promoting international peace and understanding
  Strengthening financial, economic, and political coopera-
  tion among European and Atlantic nations
  Encouraging research and greater public understanding of
  arms control and disarmament issues
  Supporting research on common problems of industrial
  societies and on the international economic order
  Assisting the relocation of political refugees, and promoting
  human rights and intellectual freedom

[10]Includes $1 million in higher education grants in Europe in addition to economic
development and administration grants in economic and social research; excludes
grants to Resources for the Future.

Improving international journalistic standards and broadcasting

Promoting interchange and cooperation among nations

Selected Major Actions:

Harvard University (arms control and international security studies) (1973–77) $ 7.0 million

United Nations (includes U.N. School, U.N. Library) (1959–77)   22.5 million

American Council of Learned Societies (American Studies) (1961–75)   10.3 million

International Association for Cultural Freedom (1956–77)   10.9 million

Council on Foreign Relations (1950–77)   6.2 million

Foreign Policy Association (1956–72)   5.2 million

14. *The Less-Developed Countries*—$919.2 million

Objectives:

Increasing food production through support of agricultural research and development of improved governmental policies

Improving the capacity of governmental and private agencies to plan and execute development programs

Supporting efforts to limit excessive population growth

Strengthening educational systems and the teaching of languages

Improving rural living standards and productivity of rural communities

Stimulating industrial and business development

Improving civil service training and governmental organization

Strengthening economic and social research on developmental issues

Strengthening research on international law and the relation of law to development, and improving legal education

Developing American university resources for overseas technical assistance

Selected Major Actions:

International agricultural research centers (1960–77)	$ 62.8 million
Population Council (1954–77)	55.2 million
Support of reproductive biology and contraceptive research (1959–77)	122.0 million
Business management and public administration in Africa, Asia, and Latin America (1959–77)	11.4 million
University development (1955–77)	38.0 million
Center for Applied Linguistics (1965–77)	6.7 million

15. *Limited Programs*

   a. *Journalism*—$10.6 million

   Objectives:

   Increasing the number of highly competent journalists, especially among minority group members

   Enabling midcareer journalists to spend a year on leave to improve their skills

   Improving the quality of journalism education

   Increasing cooperation and understanding between news media and the legal profession

   Selected Major Actions:

Advanced journalism training (Harvard, Northwestern, Stanford) (1965–69)	$4.2 million
Columbia University Graduate School of Journalism (1965)	1.6 million
Summer training program for minority journalists (1968–77)	1.4 million
"News and the Law" conferences (1974–77)	0.5 million

   b. *Aging*—$7.5 million

   Objectives:

   Stimulating new approaches to health and social services for the elderly

Developing trained personnel for local welfare services for the aged

Improving housing conditions of the elderly

Strengthening re-employment, pension, retirement programs for middle-aged and older workers

Selected Major Action:

National Social Welfare Assembly/National Council on the Aging (1957–63) $1.6 million

c. *Science*—$31.9 million

Objectives:

Increasing institutional research capacity in selected scientific fields

Supporting advanced training in the sciences

Helping develop special research facilities essential to the acceleration of discovery

Selected Major Actions:

University of Chicago (1963)	$5.0 million
Association of Universities for Research in Astronomy (1967)	5.0 million
National Academy of Sciences (1967)	5.0 million
Cornell University (1965)	4.4 million
Woods Hole Oceanographic Institution (1960–74)	.5 million

d. *Hospitals and Medical Education*—$300 million

Objectives:

Expanding or improving hospital facilites and services

Augmenting or training hospital personnel

Supporting medical research

Strengthening instruction in and financial support of U.S. medical schools

Selected Major Actions:

Privately supported hospitals (1956) $198.0 million

Endowment funds of forty-four pri-

vately supported medical schools
(1956)   90.9 million

National Fund for Medical Education
(1956)   10.0 million

e. *Michigan Philanthropies—$157.9 million*

Objectives:

Supporting Michigan-area institutions in which the
Foundation and its founders traditionally have had
an interest

Assisting promising programs and organizations likely
to benefit the Michigan community

Selected Major Actions:
Henry Ford Hospital (1950–75)	$94.8 million
Annual support to the United Foundation for Detroit charities (1940–77)	12.0 million
Edison Institute (1936–69)	39.0 million

f. *Drug Abuse—$9.1 million*

Objective:

Conducting research and analysis on problems related
to drug abuse

Major Action:
Drug Abuse Council (1972–76)	$8.8 million

g. *Philanthropy—$1.5 million*[11]

Objectives:

Conducting research on the role of philanthropy in the
context of American law and tradition

Furthering cooperation among philanthropies

Advancing public understanding of philanthropy

Major Actions:
Foundation Center (1972–76)	$500,000
Foundation Library Center (1957–61)	550,000
Russell Sage Foundation (1956–57)	225,000
University of Wisconsin (1957)	100,000

[11]Does not include grants listed under Michigan Philanthropies.

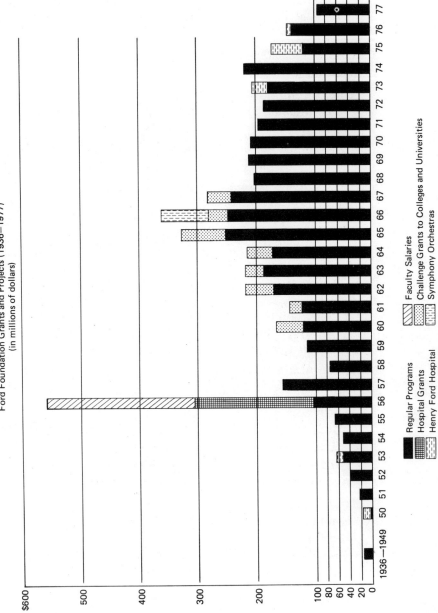

ANNUAL PROGRAM EXPENDITURES

Ford Foundation Grants and Projects (1936–1977)
(in millions of dollars)

Regular Programs
Hospital Grants
Henry Ford Hospital

Faculty Salaries
Challenge Grants to Colleges and Universities
Symphony Orchestras

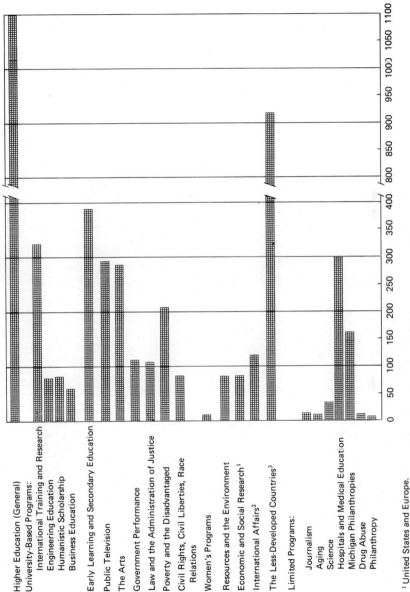

Ford Foundation Grants and Projects (1936–1977)
(in millions of dollars)

Higher Education (General)
University-Based Programs:
  International Training and Research
  Engineering Education
  Humanistic Scholarship
  Business Education

Early Learning and Secondary Education

Public Television

The Arts

Government Performance

Law and the Administration of Justice

Poverty and the Disadvantaged

Civil Rights, Civil Liberties, Race
  Relations

Women's Programs

Resources and the Environment

Economic and Social Research[1]

International Affairs[2]

The Less-Developed Countries[3]

Limited Programs:
  Journalism
  Aging
  Science
  Hospitals and Medical Education
  Michigan Philanthropies
  Drug Abuse
  Philanthropy

[1] United States and Europe.
[2] Includes foreign activities outside the less-developed countries.
[3] Includes population.

Index

195

CREDITS

Photographs: 1 — top, Homer Page; bottom, John Marmaras; 2 — top, Harvard Business School; center, the Cerro Tololo Inter-American Observatory; bottom, Roy Stevens; 3 — Roy Stevens; 4 — John Zimmerman, Black Star; 5 — top, Roy Stevens; bottom, Joe Munroe; 6 — top, Billy Barnes, The North Carolina Fund; bottom left, James Foote; bottom right, Women's Law Fund; 7 — Bedford Stuyvesant Restoration Corporation; 8 — top, Roy Stevens; bottom, Children's Television Workshop; 9 — New York City Ballet; 10 — top, Los Angeles Philharmonic; bottom, Ezra Stoller, Ulrich Franzen and Associates, Architects; 11 — top, Tim Loomis, The Nature Conservancy; bottom, Mark Godfrey, Magnum; 12 — top Ernest Kleinberg; center, Sheldon M. Machlin; bottom, Homer Page; 13 — top, Harry Redl, Black Star; bottom, Claudia Andujar Love; 14 — top, James Foote; bottom, Raghubir Singh; 15 — top, Harry Redl, Black Star; center, Karolinska Institute; bottom, James Foote. *Cartoons:* 16 — The New Yorker.